Forge The Mind

A Blueprint for Righteousness and Moral Clarity

Roylan Piloto

TruthForge Press

Library of Congress Control Number: 2025920983

ISBN: 978-1-969862-00-7

First edition — December 12, 2025

Cover design, interior design and formatting by Roylan Piloto

Printed/Manufactured in the United States of America

Before the Battle

Rules of Engagement

This book is offered for general information, spiritual encouragement, and personal reflection. It expresses the author's opinions at the time of writing and is not professional advice (including but not limited to legal, medical, psychological, financial, or therapeutic advice). Readers should consult qualified professionals regarding any decision that could affect health, safety, finances, employment, or legal standing.

Accuracy & timeliness. While reasonable efforts were made to present accurate information, facts, quotations, summaries, dates, and statistics—especially regarding current events and public figures—may change or be updated by later reporting. Any errors are unintentional. Corrections may be sent to the publisher/author for consideration in subsequent editions.

No intent to defame. Names of public figures and organizations may appear when discussing widely reported events. Inclusion does not imply endorsement or affiliation. Where conduct is described, it is based on publicly available sources and/or the author's opinion. No allegation is intended beyond what credible sources report. All persons are presumed innocent of wrongdoing unless proven otherwise in a court of law.

Quotations & Scripture. Non–Scripture quotations are attributed where used. Scripture quotations are used for devotional commentary; translation credits appear in the notes or copyright page. Biblical reflections represent the author's interpretive views.

Trademarks & fair use. All trademarks, service marks, and logos are the property of their respective owners. They are used nominatively to identify entities or works and do not indicate sponsorship or endorsement.

Anecdotes & composites. Some personal stories include composite details or adjusted timelines to protect privacy while preserving the core meaning. Any resemblance to private individuals is coincidental unless explicitly stated.

Sensitive topics. This book addresses moral, cultural, and theological issues and may critique ideas, systems, or public actions. Disagreement with an idea does not equal hostility toward persons. Readers are encouraged to examine primary sources and Scripture.

Limitation of liability. The author and publisher disclaim liability for any loss, harm, or damages arising from the use or misuse of this book. Use at your own discretion.

Endorsements. Any endorsements or reviews included are the opinions of those individuals and do not create guarantees or warranties.

Contact. For permissions, corrections, or rights inquiries, contact: truthforgepress@gmail.com

Contents

Dedication

F or my son,

Before you were born, I was already preparing this book for you—a blueprint not just of ideas, but of conviction, clarity, and the kind of strength this world cannot steal.

May this be more than pages to you. May it be a compass when you're lost, a light when the world grows dark, and a quiet voice reminding you who you are when others try to rewrite it.

Stand firm in truth. Love what is good. And never forget that your life was meant to reflect the glory of God.

You are my greatest earthly legacy. This book is part of the one I leave for you.

"Train up a child in the way he should go, and when he is old he will not depart from it."—Proverbs 22:6

Foreword

There comes a moment in every life when silence becomes betrayal—not only of others, but of yourself. This book was born from such a moment.

I wrote it to make one claim: classical virtue reaches its highest form—noble, humane and durable when ordered by the truth of Christ. I believe that claim can be tested in real life.

For years I watched truth traded for convenience, strength mocked as danger, and the image of God thinned in the hearts of men. I tried to stay polite. I tried to look away. Something in me refused.

Maybe something in you refuses too.

You've felt it—in your home, in your country, in your own mind. The world is off course. The compass is damaged. Something sacred is being treated as optional.

This isn't a manifesto for perfection. It's a call back to righteousness—not religion, not performance, not rule-stacking, but fidelity to the Good when no one is watching.

If you share my convictions, welcome. If you don't, you're still welcome. Come as a skeptic, a Stoic, a seeker, or a secular neighbor. Measure what follows not by slogans, but by reason, by Scripture, and by the kind of character it produces over time.

What follows is a field manual, not a speech. Ancient wisdom in plain words. Each chapter gives one central idea and a way to practice it—so truth is not merely admired, but lived.

Read straight through or drop into any chapter. Each stands on its own. You don't need a perfect plan to begin—just one honest step, taken today and repeated tomorrow. That is how God forges a steady soul.

Whether you're a young man trying to find purpose, a father leading a family, a woman who knows the world has lied to her, or simply someone trying to rebuild from the ashes—this book was written for you.

I don't come to impress you. I come to challenge you. And I pray that by the final page, you'll know exactly why God had you pick up this book.

"And your ears shall hear a word behind you, saying,
'This is the way, walk in it,'
when you turn to the right or when you turn to the left."—Isaiah 30:21

Introduction

Readied for the Fire

T his book began as a private blueprint—something I was building for my son. I didn't want to leave him advice that fades with mood or fashion. I wanted to leave him a path.

That path draws from three streams that belong together: the authority of Scripture, the hard-won clarity of Christian–Stoic discipline, and the tested wisdom of classical virtue. Throughout these pages you'll see them braided—Christ as the foundation, discipline as the training, virtue as the fruit.

This book is meant to be a bridge. Many respect virtue but lack Christ. Others confess Christ yet live undisciplined, without categories for forming character. A few may already have both. Most don't. Most need belief tied to backbone—truth that can be practiced, not merely affirmed.

As the pages grew, I realized I wasn't writing only for him. I was writing for anyone who feels the ground shifting—anyone watching sacred things get revised in real time, sensing the drift, and refusing to call it progress simply because it is popular. If that's you, this is for you as much as it is for him.

Here's how the path is laid out. Chapters 1–5 diagnose the fracture—how a mind loses clarity, how conscience drifts, how truth gets traded for comfort. They are written to wake you up, with early counter-moves so you don't live in analysis. Chapter 6 sets first principles: God, Logos, order—because rebuilding collapses without a definition of reality and an authority above preference. Chapters 7–12 shift from diagnosis to construction: virtue, discipline, courage, relationships, endurance, obedience. The chapters tighten as the blueprint sharpens—because diagnosis takes words; rebuilding takes action.

I won't pretend to be perfect. I've wrestled with God, failed more than once, and walked through silence and self-doubt. Yet one conviction would not die: righteousness still matters, character still counts, and truth is not negotiable even when it costs you. Self-help can adjust behavior. Christ transforms the person. This book is not about stacking rules; it is about forging a mind that can stand because a soul has bowed to the right King.

A note to skeptics: parts of this book speak directly to you on purpose. I've tried to take objections seriously, not caricature them. Where I critique, I aim to be fair. Where I claim, I invite you to verify. Read generously. Test rigorously.

We live in a loud age. Algorithms disciple more than mentors, and outrage often masquerades as courage. Therapy can name the wound; it cannot raise the dead. Stoicism can steady your breath; it cannot command the storm. What we need is older than trend and stronger than mood: a life aligned with Christ, trained by Scripture, proved under pressure.

How to Use This Book

Read slowly. Build steadily. We're after formation, not inspiration.

Read one section at a time. Don't binge; absorb.

When a Christian—Stoic Principle appears, treat it as the hinge: Scripture supplies the standard, virtue supplies the shape, practice supplies the proof. These eight principles are my own synthesis of Scripture, Stoic discipline, and classical virtue, placed where they best serve the chapter.

Each section ends with one of four anchors: Reflection, Challenge, Meditation, or Prayer.

Sit with the Reflection. Let it expose patterns and assumptions.

Act on the Challenge within twenty-four hours. Action beats intention.

Enter the Meditation without performing. Stillness trains attention, temperance, and clarity.

Pray the Prayer as written or in your own words. It's not decoration; it's alignment.

Keep a simple record—what you did, what changed, what resisted.

If reading with a spouse, friend, or group, end each session with one shared commitment. Revisit it next time.

You'll notice the through-line: Scripture first, clarity second, practice third. The goal is a mind trained to take thoughts captive, a will taught obedience, and a peace the world can neither give nor steal. Not perfection—faithfulness with traction.

If you've felt the pressure to compromise, the fatigue of trying to do right, or the ache of watching people drift from truth—you are not alone. We will confront hard things. We will tear down lies that wear friendly faces. By the end, agreement isn't my demand; strength is my aim—stronger because you wrestled, clearer because you tested, steadier because you practiced.

My son may be the reason this book exists. But if you're reading these lines, perhaps God had you in mind too. Every soul is shaped somewhere—by comfort or by fire. Here, the flames refine and the hammer restores. The forge is ready. Let's begin.

Chapter 1

The War for Your Soul

I. Opening the Gate

L ife is a crossroads, and every one of us stands before a gate—a spiritual threshold where a choice defines who we'll become. On one side lies the easy path: comfort, distraction, the pull of conformity that feels safe but leads nowhere. On the other? Challenge, growth, and a life aligned with truth. You can't straddle both worlds for long. The longer you hesitate, the harder it becomes to choose.

I've stood at that gate myself, lost in tough times when the world's noise drowned out my purpose. I binged distractions—work, screens, anything to avoid the question: Who am I becoming? This book is for anyone who's felt that same tremor—whether you're a young man searching for strength in a world of shallow role models, a woman craving truth over flattery, a parent fighting to raise kids with conviction, or a skeptic sensing there's more than politics and algorithms. That quiet discomfort you feel? It's not weakness—Don't ignore it. It may be conviction, what Scripture would call "God drawing you back".

Take Martin Luther King Jr., for example. Facing jail and death threats, he listened for that same whisper from a Birmingham cell—obeying the way he knew was right (Isaiah 30:21) despite the cost. His choice to step through the gate helped change a nation, proof that God's voice can cut through even the loudest storms. We won't face his prison cell, but we face smaller gates every day. The world trains us to sidestep the gate, to drown out purpose with noise that feels good but leaves us empty. Instead of asking, "Why am I here?" or "What does God expect of me?", we chase likes, scroll endlessly, or build identities that crumble under scrutiny. I've done it—wasted hours on screens when I knew God was calling me to more. But deep down, your soul knows when it's starving.

Righteousness isn't perfection; it's alignment—choosing what's true and good, even when it costs you. It's not a checklist for pride; it's a war cry for purpose, forged in the battles I've fought and the clarity I've found through faith. This book is here to help you forge that same clarity, whether you're standing at this gate for the first time or fighting to stay on the path.

You're at war—not just with a culture that glorifies passivity, but with the part of you tempted to settle for it. I'm writing this because I've seen that war up close, and I want you—anyone reading this, but especially someone dear to me—to win it. Before you can change the world, you must become someone who can withstand it. That means training your mind, disciplining your will, sharpening your discernment, and anchoring yourself in God's eternal truth.

This chapter's purpose is simple: to expose the war for your soul and force an honest first decision.

This path isn't easy, but it's the only one worth walking. It starts with one choice:

Step through the gate. Don't look back.

Reflection:

What's holding you back from stepping through the gate? Be honest. Not to judge yourself, but to face the mindset keeping you from the life God's calling you to.

II. The Modern Fog

The world grows louder, and its confusion grows with it. This isn't accidental. Culture manufactures the fog, media thickens it, and people who numb their moral instincts to blend in quietly accept it.

We're told that truth is relative, morality is subjective, and every person must "live their truth." But when truth loses its anchor, everything else begins to drift. As Aleksandr Solzhenitsyn warned in the wake of the Soviet collapse, evil isn't confined to a few monsters we can isolate and destroy; the line between good and evil runs through every human heart. I saw that fog firsthand in my town at a public ritual night that promised "power" but left souls empty—a story I explain later in *After the Fire*. And his warning rang true as I watched good people drift into silence and call it peace.

In the name of tolerance, we bred confusion. Behind the cry for inclusivity, we traded integrity. Under the flag of freedom, countless souls slipped into quiet bondage to vice and apathy. This isn't progress—it's decay dressed to impress.

This modern fog forms from subtle ingredients—overstimulation, comfort addiction, algorithmic dopamine, tribal outrage, spiritual apathy, and feelings elevated over facts. Together they create a haze thick enough to keep people distracted just long enough to forget they're lost.

People now treat discomfort like a disease and conviction like extremism. Righteousness is too often dismissed as judgment. Masculinity is too often labeled toxicity. Femininity is too often mocked as weakness. And truth? Too often treated like hate speech.

John Lennox once put it plainly: "What is politically correct is often not morally correct. And what is morally correct is increasingly no longer permitted."

We're no longer encouraged to sharpen our minds—only to dull our instincts. We're told that questioning the mainstream makes us dangerous. That neutrality is virtue. But neutrality in the face of evil is complicity. And silence, when righteousness is under attack, is not wisdom—it's cowardice. As Dr. King wrote from his jail cell, we often must repent not only for harsh words but for the "appalling silence of the good people."

How do you cut through this fog? Not by matching its noise—but by grounding yourself in principles that don't move, no matter how chaotic the headlines become.

Clarity doesn't rise from a scroll, a screen, or a trending podcast. It comes from honest reflection, deliberate reading, and spiritual grounding—from the quiet moments when you're alone with your thoughts, accountable before God, and willing to confront what needs correction.

Truth sets you free, but only if you desire it more than comfort.

So you begin asking the questions most people avoid:

Is what I believe actually true? Is the way I'm living consistent with that truth? Am I prepared to stand alone for what's right, even if I'm mocked?

Clarity starts when you take full ownership of your vision—and decide which voices will no longer define it.

Meditation:

Clearing the Fog
Sit still. Breathe slow.
Notice the pull toward noise, novelty, and reaction.
Name it plainly: "an impression."
Do not obey it. Do not argue with it.
Return to one sober truth: "My will is mine." Let temperance steady you until your mind stops reaching.

III. The Moral Compass

Every ship aiming for a destination must be guided by something beyond itself—a fixed point, a North Star. For the soul, that fixed point is the moral compass. But a compass only works when it's aligned with something that doesn't move.

That fixed point is God—eternal, unchanging, and perfect in righteousness. And when you are still enough to listen, you'll find God's Kingdom pressing near—present with you by His Spirit. That's where the calibration happens—not through emotion or opinion, but through divine presence and alignment.

Without that alignment, you may still move—but you'll drift. Like a captain without coordinates, you'll react to storms, chase temporary winds, and mistake speed for progress.

A well-formed moral compass is not a rigid list of rules. It's a trained sensitivity to right and wrong that becomes instinctive over time. It's shaped by wisdom, scarred by failure, and refined in silence.

One modern example is Charlie Kirk. Many people disagreed with him—sometimes strongly—but even critics could recognize this: he was willing to show up, speak plainly, and take the heat in public rather than hide behind safe silence. In a time when many trade conviction for approval, he pressed students and adults alike to engage ideas instead of censoring them. That's what a calibrated compass does under pressure: it doesn't point toward applause; it points toward what a person believes is true.

—In memory of Charlie Kirk (1993–2025)—
May our nation learn again how to argue without hatred, and stand for truth without fear.

Seneca, a Stoic philosopher, taught that virtue is the only true good. To live in virtue was to live in harmony with nature and reason—but even he, with all his insight, fell short without divine truth. The Stoics could point to the compass, but they didn't know the Source behind it.

Philosophers could glimpse the compass; Jesus revealed the Source.

Christ didn't just point—He embodied it. He said, "I am the way and the truth and the life." (John 14:6). That's not a metaphor. That's a map. And when you follow Him, your compass doesn't just warn you of evil—it draws you toward righteousness.

Today, people trade their compass for applause, pointing it toward trends instead of truth. We need men and women who live by a higher standard. Not because it's easy—but because it's right. And we test that path by a simple measure: "A just law is a man-made code that squares with the moral law—or the law of God." (MLK, *Letter from Birmingham Jail*).

Reflection:

What has shaped your current moral compass—the Word of God, or the culture around you? Take time this week to examine the roots of your convictions. Are they anchored, or are they drifting? You can't lead others if your compass isn't calibrated.

IV. The War Within

The fog of the world is tough, but the real battle? It's inside you. Your soul is a fortress, one that fractures when you try to serve two masters—truth and temptation. I've felt that split, wrestling with choices I knew were wrong, yet making them anyway in my toughest times. That tension isn't just stress or weakness—it's a spiritual war, and every one of us feels it. It didn't happen often, but every now and then the urge to waste my nights would creep up. Instead of resting, I felt it again—my thumb hovering over another scroll, another hit of distraction—while a prayer sat unfinished in my chest. I chose the easy way, slept worse, and woke up foggy. The war within is fought in tiny concessions and quiet clicks.

The Cost of a Divided Heart

Why do we feel torn? Because we straddle two worlds. You say you love righteousness, but maybe you scroll through content you know poisons your mind. You crave peace, yet hold onto grudges that steal it. You pray for clarity, but dodge the accountability God demands. That pull isn't random—it's the price of compromise. Scripture warns, "A double-minded man is unstable in all his ways" (James 1:8). That instability creeps in quietly, disguised as "just getting by," until your conscience dulls and your standards blur. I've been there, son—every honest person has chosen comfort over conviction and paid for it with inner chaos. Quick symptoms of a divided heart: (1) Private habits you'd never advise your child to copy. (2) "I'll start tomorrow" on repeat. (3) Prayerlessness when life gets busy. (4) Peace that collapses the moment the phone lights up.

The Battle Scripture Reveals

The Stoics saw this war, even without God's lens. Marcus Aurelius said, "You have power over your mind—not outside events. Realize this, and you will find strength." He was onto something true, but Scripture shows the full battlefield. Paul, no stranger to courage, confessed, "For I do not do the good I want to do, but the evil I do not want to do—this I keep on doing... What a wretched man I am! Who will rescue me from this body of death?" (Romans 7:19,24). Even Paul struggled, not with external enemies, but with his own resistance to surrender. That's the real fight—not the world's temptations, but the heart's refusal to fully obey. Victory begins where excuses end: "Thanks be to God, who delivers me through Jesus Christ our Lord!" (Romans 7:25).

From Reflection to Victory

What if you feel stuck in the struggle? You're not alone—Paul wasn't, and neither am I. Reflection helps. As a well-known proverb suggests, what you dwell on takes root. But reflection without obedience becomes avoidance. Meditation without action is like planning a battle you never fight. The war within isn't won by thinking noble thoughts—it's won by obedience, step by costly step. I held onto anger until I finally surrendered it to God. The war shifts the moment you stop negotiating with sin and start walking in what God has spoken, when the cost cuts deep. Conviction without action breeds torment; conviction with surrender brings peace. If you need a starting prayer: "Lord, show me the compromise I'm defending and the truth I'm avoiding—and give me the courage to switch sides today

Challenge:

Choose One Battle to Win;

Identify: Pinpoint one area where your actions betray your convictions—maybe it's a habit like mindless scrolling, a grudge, or dodging prayer.

Confront: Ask, "Why do I keep choosing this?"

Act: Take one concrete step toward obedience within 24 hours. Tell a trusted friend, delete that app, or pray Romans 7:24–25 for strength.

Burn the Bridge: Remove its access points—block it, replace it, commit to change.

This isn't about perfection; it's about winning one battle at a time, for you and for the life God's calling you to lead.

V. Voices in the Storm

In every generation, truth is under siege—not only by force, but by volume. The storm doesn't always come as open persecution. Sometimes it comes as distraction, noise, or the constant hum of narratives designed to keep you spiritually dull. Noise is a bully; you beat it with boundaries.

Most people don't fall because they hate truth. They fall because they can't hear it anymore. It's drowned out by talking heads, trends, peer pressure, and inner dialogue that's never been challenged. Eventually, silence becomes more comfortable than clarity. But clarity requires courage—especially when the truth you're called to speak isn't popular. The week I muted nothing, my courage shrank with my attention span. The week I muted almost everything, the Word rose above the noise again.

We live in an age where everyone has a platform, but few have a voice. Many echo. Few speak from conviction. You can't follow every voice and expect to remain rooted in truth.

Jesus warned us of this: "My sheep listen to my voice; I know them, and they follow Me." (John 10:27). That wasn't just about comfort—it was about discernment. There are many voices in the world, but only one that leads to life.

Dr. Frank Turek often says that truth will inevitably offend someone; the real question is whether we fear offending people more than offending God.

The storm around you is not neutral. Every voice is shaping you—forming beliefs, habits, and instincts. That's why Scripture tells us to "take every thought captive" and test every spirit. (2 Corinthians 10:5; 1 John 4:1). If you don't guard your inputs, you'll eventually lose your discernment. Use this "Shepherd Test": Does this voice push me toward humility, repentance, and courage—or toward outrage, flattery, and fear? If it thrives on my anxiety, it isn't the Shepherd.

Practice—Mute • Script • Schedule:

Mute: Unfollow, block, or silence three accounts that spike envy, fear, or lust.

Script: Pre-write a 1–2 sentence response you'll use when pressured to echo a view you don't hold (e.g., "I care about people too much to lie to them. Here's what I believe...").

Schedule: Create two daily silence windows (5–10 minutes) for Scripture and prayer. Put them on your calendar like meetings.

Sometimes the most radical thing you can do is turn off the noise—not because silence is safe, but because it allows you to hear the voice of God again.

And once you've heard Him clearly, you'll never settle for noise again.

Reflection:

What voices have you allowed to shape your thinking? This week, fast from one source of noise—a show, a podcast, an influencer, or an opinion feed. Replace it with quiet study, worship, or prayer. Let God's voice rise above the world's. Measure it: cut your daily inputs by 50% for seven days and track two numbers—minutes in Scripture and minutes in passive media. Watch which number predicts your peace.

VI. The Path of Righteousness

The voices of the world can drown out truth, but there's a path that cuts through the noise—a trail forged by righteousness. This isn't a badge you wear; it's a direction you choose—a path that demands a destination, a map, and the courage to keep walking no matter how rough the ground gets. From the student navigating peer pressure to the parent striving to lead with integrity to the seeker pursuing real purpose, this path is for you.

Alignment Over Appearance

I still remember a season with a friend who was like a brother—choosing image over integrity by defending myself instead of listening. He was often wrong—at least that's what I told myself—I enjoyed being right more than listening to him. When he called out something I could do better, I'd dismantle the point and feel peace evaporate overnight; only when I meditated and sincerely apologized the path reappeared. Righteousness is how you find your way back—not by winning arguments, but by letting God make you right, one obedient step at a time. Too many confuse righteousness with reputation—looking good instead of being good. But this path isn't about applause; it's about alignment—with truth, with God's Word, with the purpose you were created for. The world shouts, "Be true to yourself!" Scripture counters, "Deny yourself" (Luke 9:23). The world says, "Do what feels good." God says, do what is good, even when it hurts. I've faced that choice—clinging to pride when humility would've set me free—and I want better for you, for anyone ready to walk this trail.

The Narrow Way

Why is the path narrow? Not because God's cruel, but because truth doesn't bend. It calls you upward, not inward, starting not with performance but with surrender. What's harder than bowing in humility? I've struggled with that, resisting God's call to let go of my own plans. But every step on this path is a choice—you don't inherit righteousness; you choose it, one decision at a time. And you're not alone. Christ blazed this trail, not in comfort but through betrayal, rejection, and the cross. He didn't dodge suffering; He embraced it, carving a way for us to follow.

Clarity Over Comfort

What if the way ahead feels too steep? That's where faith takes over. You don't need perfection, only direction. The goal isn't comfort; it's clarity. I chased the world's version of "good" and wound up empty, but God's road, though harder, gave my life weight and aim. Let the culture chase its momentary highs. You, fighting inner battles or guiding those behind you—stand in the same line as the saints, the prophets, and your Savior.

Reflection:

Identify: Write down one area where your choices clash with your values—maybe chasing approval over integrity or avoiding a tough stand.

Ask: What's pulling me off God's path? Pray Luke 9:23 for strength.

Act: Take one small step today—apologize, say no to a temptation, or commit to a godly habit.

Your path starts now. Choose clarity, and keep walking.

VII. The Power of Discipline

Discipline isn't just a character trait—it's a spiritual weapon. It guards the gates of your mind, reinforces your values, and strengthens your ability to choose what's right over what's easy.

In the absence of discipline, desire becomes the dictator. You do what feels good instead of what is good. And slowly, the mind loses its grip on reality and righteousness alike.

Proverbs says, "Like a city whose walls are broken through is a person who lacks self-control." (Proverbs 25:28). That's not poetic exaggeration—it's a warning. A life without discipline is vulnerable to every temptation, every trend, every emotional high and crash.

We now live in a culture that mocks self-restraint and glorifies indulgence. People boast about their impulsivity like it's freedom, when in truth, it's bondage with a filter. We swipe, scroll, and snack our way through discomfort instead of confronting it—and then wonder why we feel spiritually empty. A 9 p.m. phone curfew can feel like withdrawal at first—then it starts to feel like freedom.

David Goggins, a former Navy SEAL, once said, "You have to build calluses on your mind." He wasn't speaking biblically, but the principle holds. Discipline builds resilience. It conditions the will to obey when the body or emotions protest.

But biblical discipline isn't about brute strength. It's about devotion. It's the ability to submit your instincts to your calling. To say no to what feels urgent, so you can say yes to what's eternal.

The disciplined mind doesn't avoid struggle—it embraces it as training. Because every act of self-control sharpens your soul and prepares you for the real battles—the ones that don't come with warnings.

You'll never regret being disciplined. But you'll often regret being ruled by impulse.

Reflection:

What's one area in your life where a lack of discipline is quietly weakening you? This week, choose one discipline to develop—waking up earlier, resisting a distraction, committing to prayer or study—and follow through. Build spiritual calluses. Strength begins with a single repetition.

Practice—Build Discipline in 7 Days: (1) Pick one keystone habit (bedtime, Bible, or breathwork). (2) Set a 2-minute "minimum viable" version so you can't skip. (3) Add friction to the competing habit (move the app, block the site, put phone outside room). (4) Track it daily with a simple ☐. (5) On day 7, raise the bar slightly and choose your next keystone.

VIII. Training the Will

The will is like a muscle. It doesn't grow through hope—it grows through use. And like any muscle, it must be trained intentionally, not just when it's convenient.

You will not become righteous by accident. You must decide, in advance, what you will stand for—and then train your will to follow through. Without this preparation, you'll break under pressure. And when your will breaks, your integrity follows.

It started with a quiet promise I kept breaking: "Bible before phone." Most mornings I meant it; too many mornings I didn't. The day I wrote it down, set a phone timer, and told my wife my plan, the follow-through finally stuck.

Jesus said, "The spirit is willing, but the flesh is weak." (Matthew 26:41). He didn't say that to shame us—He said it to warn us. Even noble intentions collapse without practiced obedience.

The Stoics understood this. Epictetus taught that "no man is free who is not master of himself." But self-mastery doesn't mean you're led by pride—it means you're governed by principle. And principles require preparation.

When you fail to train your will, you default to instinct. And instincts—while useful in survival—are dangerous in morality. They'll convince you that fear is wisdom, lust is love, and silence is strength. So you rehearse a better instinct on purpose.

You must decide ahead of time how you will respond to temptation, pressure, and confusion. Not in theory—but in practice. Write "if–then" scripts you can use under load: *If* I feel the scroll urge at night, *then* I plug my phone in the kitchen and open to a Psalm. *If* anger spikes, *then* I breathe for ten seconds and say, "Lord, help," before I speak.

Your mind will never stay neutral. If you don't fill it with truth on purpose, lies will move in by default. That includes your will. If it isn't pre-trained to obey truth, it will default to serving comfort.

So how do you train the will? You decide before the moment comes. You resolve—daily, quietly, without applause—to obey in small ways that compound over time. Choose now that you won't lie when the truth costs you. Decide you'll walk away from temptation instead of flirting with it. Commit to pray before panic sets in, to hold your peace when anger flares, and to honor God when no one's watching. These aren't dramatic gestures—they're pre-decisions that build strength.

Then practice them: take three short, intentional rehearsals today. Say the commitment out loud. Picture the moment. Take one small step—move the phone, draft the text, set the timer.

Your will doesn't grow in the spotlight. It's forged in quiet choices that no one sees but God.

Meditation:

The Keystone
Lower the shoulders. Ease the jaw.
Picture your character like a structure: one weak beam strains the whole house.
Choose one small discipline that strengthens the frame.
Wisdom does not demand drama—it asks for consistency.
Rest your mind on this: "Virtue grows by repetition."

IX. Building Inner Peace in a Loud World

Peace isn't found—it's forged. And in a world obsessed with noise, you won't stumble into it by accident. You must build it deliberately, with intention and discipline.

Too many confuse numbness with peace. They numb out for hours—noise, feeds, and harmless-looking escapes—and call it rest. But rest isn't escape—it's restoration. And peace is not the absence of noise. It's the presence of God in the midst of it. For me it started with five quiet minutes at the kitchen table—coffee steaming, phone in the other room—reading one Psalm and sitting still. The room didn't change; my spirit did.

The prophet Isaiah wrote, "You will keep in perfect peace those whose minds are steadfast, because they trust in You." (Isaiah 26:3). Notice the source: not environment, not circumstance, but trust—and steadfastness of mind.

Peace isn't passive. It's a byproduct of alignment. When your life aligns with truth—when your habits align with your values, and your values align with God—peace becomes the atmosphere of your soul. You don't wait for calm; you practice it until it becomes your baseline.

Marcus Aurelius wrote, "Nowhere can man find a quieter or more untroubled retreat than in his own soul." But that's only true if the soul has been trained to host peace—not chaos, fear, or guilt. The world offers noise disguised as clarity. It's up to you to guard what enters your mind. Guardrails matter: curfew for screens, a rule for mornings ("Scripture before feeds"), and a weekly hour of device-free work or worship.

Your soul is your responsibility. And if you don't build a peaceful spirit, the world will give you a restless one by default.

The loudest storm cannot shake a grounded soul. But an ungrounded soul will crumble, even in silence.

Practice—Build a Quiet Core (PEACE):

P—Prepare the space: phone out of room; timer 5 minutes.

E—Exhale: slow breaths (in 4, hold 4, out 6) for one minute.

A—Attend to Scripture: read one Psalm or Gospel paragraph, out loud.

C—Converse with God: two honest sentences: gratitude + request.

E—Examine: write one line on what changed (anxiety down? clarity up?).

Prayer:

Lord Jesus, I lay down the noise I have chosen and the restlessness I have fed. Calm what is frantic in me. Clean what is crowded in me. Teach me to guard my peace without becoming passive, and to be still without becoming lazy. Make my mind sober, my heart steady, and my attention obedient. Let Your truth anchor me deeper than the storm can reach. Amen.

X. Forging Conviction

Conviction isn't emotion—it's endurance. It's what keeps a man anchored when the culture around him collapses. And it's not built in a moment of passion, but in moments of resolve—repeatedly. Conviction grows in quiet repetitions long before the spotlight ever finds you.

Conviction is what made Stephen preach as stones flew at his skull. It's what drove Paul to write letters from a prison cell instead of giving up. It's what led Christ to the cross, when He could have summoned angels.

Without conviction, truth becomes a costume—worn for applause, discarded under pressure. But with conviction, truth becomes your spine.

I learned this at a late meeting when a leader suggested we "soften" the truth to keep a client happy. I felt the pull to keep my image intact and the room calm. I closed the laptop instead and told the truth. We lost favor that night. I slept in peace. Conviction didn't make the moment easier; it made my footing sure.

We live in a generation that praises passion but avoids pressure. Passion is loud. Conviction is quiet—until it's tested. And when it's tested, it's revealed for what it really is. Testing only reveals what training already built.

You don't need to be loud to be unshakable. You need to be clear, consistent, and anchored. The enemy isn't threatened by noise—he's threatened by the man who refuses to bend.

Tim Keller pictured prayer like this: only a child dares wake a king at 3 a.m. for water—and in Christ, we have that kind of access. That's the kind of conviction that comes from knowing who you belong to—and living like it.

Conviction isn't just believing something—it's being transformed by it. It's letting truth shape your choices when it costs you comfort, relationships, or recognition.

And if you want to lead others, you must first be led by conviction yourself. Because people don't follow charisma forever—they follow consistency.

Challenge:

Define Your Non-Negotiables
1) Ground: Write three convictions from Scripture (one verse each) you will not bend on.
2) Resolve: Pre-decide one sentence you'll speak when each is

tested.

3) Rehearse: Say those sentences out loud today—twice.

4) Expose: Tell one trusted person your three and invite accountability.

5) Review: In seven days, note where you held or folded, and adjust.

XI. The Hidden Cost of Delay

The world's noise and your inner battles set the stage, but there's a subtler enemy—one that's wrecked more lives than failure or fear. It doesn't shout or threaten; it whispers, sounding reasonable, even wise: I'll change later. I fell for that lie once, putting off a hard choice during my darkest days, thinking tomorrow would be easier. It wasn't. That delay cost me clarity, and I don't want that for you.

The Thief of Conviction

Later" is a thief—it steals conviction and buries good intentions in a graveyard. The enemy doesn't need to crush your faith; he only needs you to wait. Scripture makes the cost unmistakable: Pharaoh delayed obedience, hardening his heart with every refusal to release Israel and inviting greater judgment each time. Felix, the Roman governor, heard Paul's message, trembled, and replied, "When I find it convenient, I will send for you" (Acts 24:25). He never did. Their delays didn't just postpone change—they calcified the heart. Delay doesn't make you stronger; it makes you numb. Each "not yet" trains your soul to resist the very light that could heal it.

What about you? What's the one thing you're avoiding because it feels too heavy? I've delayed too—skipping a needed apology, postponing prayer—convincing myself I'd be ready later. But postponement doesn't forge strength; it forms resistance. God speaks not for admiration, but alignment. Every moment you delay what is right, you strengthen the part of you that opposes righteousness and let it rise to the throne.

Readiness isn't an emotion you wait for; it's a muscle built by obeying once.

Act Now, or Drift Forever

What if you're not ready? That's the trap—waiting for "ready" when obedience builds readiness. Scripture warns believers, not just rebels: "Today, if you hear his voice, do not harden your hearts" (Hebrews 3:15). Delay doesn't just stall discipline; it clouds the clarity you're fighting for. I learned this the hard way, son—when I put off God's call and drifted further from peace.

Challenge:

Act Before "Later"
Name it (2 lines): Write the one act you keep delaying and why.
Shrink it (10 minutes): take the smallest honest step now (draft the text, set the timer, open the Bible).
Remove friction: delete the shortcut that feeds delay (app, bookmark, late-night cue).
Tell one person: send a one-sentence commitment and ask for a check-in tomorrow.
Close the loop: before bed, record "did/didn't" and one sentence on what you'll do differently.

XII. The Decision Point—The War for Your Soul

This is not a closing message—it's a turning point.
You're not being invited into a lifestyle brand or a new set of habits.
You're being called to war—a spiritual war.
And the contested territory is your soul.
    Everything you've read so far has been preparation for a decision. But now the choice is yours:
Will you return to passivity—or will you stand and fight?
Not through violence, but through virtue.

Not with anger, but with obedience.

Not to impress, but to align.

You are a person of infinite worth—created in the image of God, designed with purpose, and equipped for victory.

But none of that matters if you choose neutrality.

Jesus didn't die so you could admire Him at a distance.

He died to purchase your freedom—and to call you into battle for others.

The Gospel is not a retreat.

It's a declaration of war against darkness, lukewarm compromise, and the lies that have ruled too many lives for too long.

And now, that declaration rests in your hands.

Choose your side. Raise your discipline. Forge your mind.

And when the world asks who sent you—tell them the truth: The King did.

Challenge:

Take the Oath

Write (2–3 lines): your vow—not a goal. A vow.

Name: what you will stand for, who you will become, and what you will no longer tolerate in yourself.

Seal (within 24 hours): take one visible act that matches your vow.

Tell: share it with one trusted witness who will check in tomorrow.

Set the watch: choose a 30-day review date and keep it.

Chapter 2

The Collapse of Virtue

I. A Generation Without Anchors

T he world spins faster, but we're adrift—cut loose from the anchors of faith, family, and truth. I felt this drift in my darkest season. For weeks, I traded morning prayers for newsfeeds, chasing validation in endless debates and mistaking movement for meaning. The aftermath is predictable: attention splinters, peace thins, and purpose fades into noise. That inner unrest you feel—that gnawing sense that something is off, that life was meant to be deeper—is your soul crying out for an eternal anchor. Maybe you're exhausted, confused, or quietly hungry for something real. Collapse accelerates when minds conform; recovery begins when minds renew (Romans 12:2).

The Shattered Foundation

We're drowning in data—posts, opinions, feeds—but wisdom starves. Virtue, once a mark of strength, is mocked as oppression. Truth, our compass, is dismissed as "your truth." Identity, meant to reflect God's image, fractures into confusion. A.W. Tozer warned, "If you do not worship God, you will worship something—likely yourself." I've been there, chasing self over God, only to crash. The world trades faith for slogans, family for screens, truth for feelings. Without anchors, you don't stand—you sink.

A Biblical Mirror

Scripture saw this coming: "There arose another genera-tion... who did not know the Lord" (Judges 2:10). Israel didn't fall from ignorance but from forsaking their anchors, sliding into idolatry and decay. Sound familiar? We're not just losing facts—we're abandoning truth. C.S. Lewis said, "We make men without chests and expect from them virtue and enterprise." History echoes the pattern: prosperity softens courage, plea-sure replaces purpose, and a people drift. Rome rotted from excess even as a stubborn church in that city learned to live anchored. God always keeps a remnant—men like Daniel in exile and believers who refuse the drift.

Reclaiming What's Lost

If you feel adrift, you're not lost—you're called. That spark in you knows substance from noise, freedom from slavery. I drifted too, but God's truth pulled me back. This isn't de-spair—it's a diagnosis. You can rebuild. Name one anchor you've let slip—faith, family, integrity—and reclaim it today for your-self, for someone you love, for a world watching.

Prayer:

Father, restore my anchors. Where I have drifted from truth, pull me back. Where I have neglected what matters, renew my love. Re-root me in Your Word and make me steady. Amen.

II. What Is Virtue?

Virtue isn't a trend you chase or a hashtag you slap on a post. It's moral excellence—proved in sacrifice and aligned with God's unchanging truth. It's the compass that points to righteous-ness, not applause. Daniel learned this in Babylon: he was of-fered comfort, status, and a quiet path of compromise—and he "resolved" not to defile himself (Daniel 1:8). No speech. No spotlight. Just a private decision that kept his soul anchored when everything around him tried to pull it loose.

The ancients knew virtue mattered. Aristotle called it the golden mean—balance honed by habit, not whim. But he only saw part of the map. In the biblical sense, virtue runs deeper than self-control; it is formation: surrender to God's righteousness and daily practice. Peter urges us to add virtue to faith (2 Peter 1:5) because belief alone won't hold under pressure. Faith must become visible in choices—day in, day out—especially when no one is watching. That is mind renewal in motion (Romans 12:2).

Today, we flatten virtue into niceness, courage into tolerance, and discipline into self-care. The world says your feelings are truth and discomfort is the enemy. But real virtue walks into the hard stuff—confronting lies, rejecting vice, and saying no to what degrades the soul. A virtuous man may not be liked, but he becomes trustworthy. A virtuous woman may not chase trends, but she stands when others fold. Virtue isn't the easy path—it's the path that leads to peace: the kind you feel when you're right with God, even if the world resists you for it.

Reflection:

Where have you chosen comfort over virtue in the past week—a lie you let slide, a temptation you indulged? What would it cost to align that choice with God's truth? Pray 2 Peter 1:5 (and echo Romans 12:2) and ask Him to show you.

III. Virtue Requires Strength and Sacrifice

The modern world loves the idea of virtue—but not its Source. We want kindness without truth, compassion without conviction, justice without judgment. We talk about "doing the right thing" while rejecting the foundation that defines what right is. Without God, virtue becomes a moving target—renamed by each culture, trend, or personal whim.

Christian–Stoic Principle #2—Virtue Is the Only True Good; Store Treasures in Heaven

Classical virtue ethics held a hard line: wealth, reputation, comfort, and pleasure are unstable, but character can be steady. External conditions change. A man can lose money and keep integrity. He can lose status and keep courage. He can be hated and still act justly. In that sense, the point stands: if your "goodness" depends on what the world gives, the world can take it away.

That tradition called many externals "indifferent"—not meaningless, but not ultimate. Some are preferred (health, stability, provision). Some are destructive (addiction, cruelty, cowardice). The wisdom is simple: pursue what is reasonable, but never worship it. Comfort can be enjoyed, but it cannot be obeyed.

Scripture elevates the foundation. Moral excellence is not merely "useful," "noble," or "reasonable." It is goodness aligned with the character and authority of God. Without Him, the word "good" eventually collapses into preference. And once there is no standard above man, everything becomes subjective—and when everything is subjective, power decides what is "good." That isn't morality; it's manipulation.

Even when people deny God, they still borrow from His reality. Conscience, moral outrage, and the instinct that some things are truly wrong are not accidents—they are echoes of a Lawgiver. But when a culture rejects that Lawgiver, righteousness gets replaced by appetite, ego, and ideological force.

Some thinkers embraced this openly. Nietzsche mocked Christian virtue as weakness and pushed will-to-power instead: create your own values, rule by strength, and use moral language as a tool. Set beside Christ, the contrast is stark: Nietzsche preached self-creation; Christ "emptied Himself" in obedience (Philippians 2:5–8). One exalts will; the other reveals truth. One produces winners and casualties; the other produces saints. This is what happens when man plays god—he becomes a tyrant, even over himself.

The Bible warned of the same progression long ago: "Claiming to be wise, they became fools... and worshiped created things rather than the Creator" (Romans 1:22–23). When goodness is divorced from God, a society may keep the vocabulary but lose the substance. It may talk about justice and forget mercy. It may celebrate tolerance and abandon truth. It may preach love and strip it of its meaning.

True virtue doesn't arise from human willpower alone. It flows from the nature of God. He does not merely approve what is true—He is true. He does not merely require justice—He is just. And because God is unchanging, goodness is not up for vote.

That is why Jesus taught you to store treasure where theft can't reach: "Lay up for yourselves treasures in heaven... For where your treasure is, there your heart will be also" (Matthew 6:20–21). The Christian–Stoic man measures success by faithfulness, not applause; by righteousness, not reward. Money, comfort, and recognition are gifts—never gods. Virtue is the only treasure anchored past the grave—and in Christ, it becomes evidence of a life being redeemed.

Reflection:

Where have you tried to live morally while sidelining God? Ask yourself: Is my pursuit of virtue rooted in surrender to God—or in performance, pride, or cultural approval?

IV. The Algorithms of the Age

We like to think we're free. But freedom has become a performance, and the stage is owned by systems designed to shape attention. In the age of algorithms, attention is currency—and someone else is cashing in. Every scroll, swipe, and click feeds a machine that doesn't merely predict your behavior; it trains it. Slowly, your preferences become your habits, and your habits become your prison.

Algorithms don't just learn what you like—they learn what weakens you. They reward outrage to keep you reactive, lust to keep you hooked, and vanity to keep you insecure. That isn't freedom; it's engineering.

Look around. The incentives favor impulse and novelty over reflection and wisdom. Filters distort beauty until even the confident feel inadequate. Rage cycles and moral grandstanding get amplified because they keep you engaged. Over time, attention splinters, peace thins, and the soul forgets how to sit still—how to pray, how to think, how to be present.

"In their own eyes they flatter themselves too much to detect or hate their sin." (Psalm 36:2). David's warning exposes the same danger: self-trust feels righteous in the moment, yet blinds the heart to its own ruin.

When we delegate our curiosity to algorithms, we surrender agency. When we numb pain with noise, we never heal. And when we chase only what's pleasurable, we lose our appetite for what's meaningful.

This isn't oppression through force—it's sedation through pleasure. Bread and circuses once pacified Rome. Today it's dopamine on demand. The enemy no longer needs to hide in shadows—he can keep you busy, entertained, and spiritually dull.

If you don't program your mind, something else will.

Meditation:

Breaking the Algorithm
Sit in silence and watch the first impulse.
Does it chase outrage, comparison, or escape?
Pause before you assent.
Wisdom begins in the gap between stimulus and response.
Choose one thought that makes you more truthful, more calm, more just—and keep it there.

V. The Enemy of Virtue Is Vice

Virtue is not just the presence of good habits—it is active resistance to vice. And in today's world, vice isn't hiding. It's trending.

What once crept in quietly now parades proudly. The shame that once protected conscience has been replaced by applause for rebellion. Our world doesn't merely tolerate sin—it often promotes it, decorates it, and demands you celebrate it.

Vice begins in small compromises. A little indulgence here. A rationalization there. Before long, convictions erode, conscience dulls, and the soul starts negotiating with what it once fled. This is how civilizations collapse—not in one cataclysm, but in a thousand shrugs.

"The safest road to hell is the gradual one—the gentle slope, soft underfoot, without sudden turnings, without milestones, without signposts."—C.S. Lewis

We are now a culture addicted to vice, and that addiction is being monetized. Pornography is normalized, even marketed as "empowerment." Exploitation is rebranded as opportunity. Rage media sells division as courage. Nihilistic humor numbs pain but never heals it. Influencers preach self-worship under the name of authenticity. And all of it—every click, every impulse—is designed to keep you distracted, disarmed, and spiritually weak.

"A man who does not actively resist vice will eventually serve it."

This is not paranoia—it's pattern recognition. I learned this young. In high school, "health talks" treated pornography like neutral information; curiosity cracked the door. By my early twenties, I cut it off. God spared me from a horrible situation before it became one, and by grace I never looked back. "Walk by the Spirit, and you will not gratify the desires of the flesh" (Galatians 5:16).

Vice doesn't feel dangerous at first. That's the trap. It feels like relief. Like freedom. But it's slavery with a friendly face. And the longer you let it stay, the more it grows. What begins as private indulgence becomes public consequence. What you tolerate in secret today becomes your reputation tomorrow—or worse, your child's inheritance. Scripture shows both endings: Sodom normalized vice and was judged; Nineveh confessed and was spared. There is always a Nineveh option.

Vice is never satisfied with permission. It wants ownership. It won't just damage your future—it will reshape your desires and warp your identity.

That's why virtue must be trained like a soldier and guarded like a gate. No one drifts into righteousness. You pursue it through discipline—fasting, prayer, confession, boundaries, resistance—especially when it cuts deep, and all the more because it does.

Challenge:

Cut One Root

Identify: Name one vice you've excused (lust, anger, envy, pride, escapism). Write the sentence you use to justify it.

Map: Write the three most common triggers (time, place, emotion).

Break: Remove one access point today (device boundary, location, relationship pattern, private routine). Make it specific.

Replace: Pre-decide one righteous response for each trigger (walk outside, cold water, Scripture, text a brother, serve someone, go to bed).

Expose: Tell one trusted person the vice and the trigger map. Ask them to check in at one set time each day for 7 days.

Review: After 7 days, write what trigger was strongest and what replacement actually worked—then tighten the plan.

VI. Virtue Begins in Private

The world celebrates public success, but the soul is built in secret. Virtue isn't formed under spotlights—it is proven in the moments when no one is watching. Character grows in unseen places long before it becomes visible anywhere else.

Who you are behind closed doors says more about your integrity than what you post, wear, or accomplish. We live in an age of performance: men curate an image online while neglecting the heart offline. It's easy to appear righteous. It's harder to be righteous.

True virtue demands consistency—not only in the face of applause, but in the silence of daily choices. It shows up in your tone with your wife when no one hears, in what you watch when you think no one knows, in how you treat your children, your parents, your God—not only in moments of pressure, but in the habits that make up your private life.

What you tolerate in secret eventually shapes you in public. A man who lies to himself long enough stops noticing. He may convince others, but he loses the mirror of his own soul. Secrecy is fertilizer for sin; light is its poison.

"Nothing is hidden that will not be made manifest, nor is anything secret that will not be known and come to light." (Luke 8:17)

You can't build a righteous life on a foundation of secrets. One hidden crack will eventually split the structure. The enemy doesn't need to destroy you publicly—he only needs to corrupt you privately. Once rot sets in, collapse becomes a timetable. This isn't about perfection; it's about truth—to God and to yourself.

The man who begins the journey of virtue must be willing to face his shadow and invite the light in. That takes humility. That takes courage. But it's where real strength is born. I learned this in a season of quiet failure—carrying resentment at home—until confession cut it at the root and the old prayer rose again:

"Create in me a clean heart, O God" (Psalm 51:10). Your Father who sees in secret already knows. Private surrender isn't weakness—it's the training ground of unshakable character.

The men who shaped history with integrity were disciplined in secret long before they carried influence. Their legacies didn't start on platforms. They started in prayer closets, handwritten pages, quiet confessions, and consistent decisions.

Private virtue builds public legacy. And every man must choose: will I chase image, or pursue integrity? Choose integrity, and hidden faithfulness will echo through generations—outshining any spotlight.

Reflection:

If someone could see a hidden camera of your last 24 hours—not your words, but your habits, your thoughts, your time—would they still call you a righteous man? If not, what needs to change in the quiet? Write it plainly, then pray Psalm 51:10 and take one small act of obedience today.

VII. The Surrender of Self-Control

A culture without self-control is in free fall. We're told to "do what feels right," "trust your truth," and "indulge your desires"—as if impulse is wisdom and craving is identity. But self-control has always been the boundary between chaos and order, slavery and strength. Without it, a man becomes governed by appetite—and eventually undone by it.

You don't have to look far to see the pattern: addiction is excused, indulgence celebrated, prudence called oppression, debt normalized, impulse marketed as authenticity, and discipline branded "toxic." In a world like that, losing self-control doesn't look like rebellion—it looks like belonging.

This isn't accidental. It's spiritual. When self-control collapses, virtue becomes impossible—because the flesh doesn't drift

THE COLLAPSE OF VIRTUE   37

toward righteousness. It must be trained. And if you won't train it, the world will tempt it until it owns you.

I felt this pull when I binged a show past midnight, ignoring my family's need for rest—trading dominion for distraction. As C.S. Lewis warned, repeated surrender to impulse dulls the will and eventually dulls the heart.

The Apostle Paul didn't treat self-control as a helpful tip—he called it a fruit of the Spirit (Galatians 5:23). That means it isn't optional. It's essential. Without it, love becomes lust. Kindness becomes cowardice. Peace becomes passivity. And eventually, faith becomes fantasy. Esau traded a birthright for a bowl; Joseph refused a bed and gained a legacy—two futures decided by temperance.

In the digital age, your will is constantly provoked. Platforms are engineered to override restraint. Notifications tug. Ads prime. Feeds are tuned to reflex. If you don't train your will, it softens—and the flesh wins without a fight.

But here's the truth: you are not a slave to desire. You are a soul with dominion. You weren't made to obey every urge, but to rule them. Self-control isn't repression—it's redemption. Discipline doesn't exist to make you suffer; it exists to declare, "My spirit leads—not lust, ego, or fear." It tells the body, "You don't run the house; the Lord does." And every time a lesser craving receives a no, a greater calling receives a yes. Train now, and your legacy will endure.

Challenge:

Own Your Impulse
Name & trigger: Identify one arena (screen time, speech, temper, appetite) and the moment it hits.
Train (10 min): Choose one practice today that bows that urge to truth (e.g., Scripture before screen; a two-minute pause before reply; water + walk before snack).
Tell: Text a friend for accountability.
Track (7 days): Rate strength 1–5 nightly; note where resistance grows easier.

VIII. The Rejection of Responsibility

Where responsibility dies, freedom follows. What replaces it is not liberty, but chaos wearing a mask.

We are watching a shift from ownership to blame, from duty to entitlement, from "What must I do?" to "What am I owed?" This isn't empathy. It's erosion.

We no longer train people to carry burdens; we train them to outsource them. We explain instead of own: children blame parents, students blame teachers, citizens blame systems. Everyone has a story. Few want to take responsibility for the ending.

When responsibility collapses, resentment takes its place. Resentment breeds fragility, disorder, and rage—not only in individuals, but across generations.

"The purpose of life is finding the largest burden that you can bear and bearing it."—Jordan B. Peterson

That isn't punishment. It's meaning.

Responsibility came before the fall: "The Lord God took the man and put him in the garden of Eden to work it and keep it" (Genesis 2:15). God did not make man for ease. He made him for stewardship. That hasn't changed.

Empathy matters. But empathy without ownership hardens into excuse.

I learned this at home. I blamed "a busy week" for a promise I broke. I dropped the excuse and owned it. The room softened. Responsibility puts your hands back on the wheel.

Our age has written a theology of blame: "You're not responsible." "It's society's fault." "Your pain justifies your passivity." None of that leads to peace. It produces powerlessness. Then powerlessness becomes identity.

Responsibility restores dignity. It is the weight that makes a man strong, the burden that builds the backbone of a household. It begins where excuses end. "Each one should carry their own load... for each will have to give an account" (Galatians 6:5).

Embrace responsibility and three things happen: you stop waiting for rescue; you start building what lasts; you become trustworthy—to others and before God. The weight you choose to carry today becomes the legacy your children inherit tomorrow. This is not about carrying everything. It is about carrying what is yours.

Challenge:

Own One Load
Name (1 line): The sphere you've avoided (family, faith, finances, health).
Act today: One concrete deliverable you will complete without blame.
Tell: Text one person your commitment for accountability.
Review (7 days): Note results and name the next load to shoulder.

IX. The Decline of Discipline

Discipline is not glamorous. It doesn't trend. It rarely earns applause. Yet it is the hidden force behind every worthy achievement, every moral victory, every lasting legacy.

When discipline collapses, virtue doesn't disappear in a day. It erodes—quietly, steadily, through a thousand excuses.

Modern society sells shortcuts. Apps promise change without effort. Diets promise results without restraint. Standards get lowered to spare feelings. Pop culture calls self-control "toxic." The message is consistent: avoid strain, avoid discomfort, avoid cost.

But righteousness has a price. If you refuse to train, you will not endure. No greatness without discipline. No mastery. No peace. No clarity.

"No man is more unhappy than he who never faces adversity. For he is not permitted to prove himself."—Seneca

Adversity is the furnace. Discipline is the iron.

You don't sharpen your soul in comfort; you sharpen it in resistance. Even Christ modeled this: before His ministry, He fasted forty days. No crowd. No applause. Hunger, isolation, temptation—obedience. Not ritual. Preparation. He who had all authority still submitted His body to the will of the Father. Preparation before platform. That is the standard.

Our age treats discipline like oppression. The man who wakes early, denies himself, and commits to purpose is called rigid. The man who drifts into indulgence is praised as "free." But freedom without discipline is chaos in disguise.

Competence isn't gifted. It's forged—in early mornings, in delayed gratification, in showing up when no one claps, in doing the right thing when you feel nothing.

I've failed here. I've made excuses, taken shortcuts, justified laziness. It always costs more than it saves. The bill comes due in weakness, regret, and lost trust. The undisciplined life looks easier, but it robs the soul of strength and quietly rots potential from within.

Discipline isn't optional. It's the price of becoming trustworthy. You can't be a strong father, a good leader, a reliable man without it. You can't speak truth in a loud world if you haven't trained your tongue, your time, and your desires.

Discipline doesn't reveal itself in grand moments. It's built in small, uncelebrated ones. And it's never too late to reclaim it.

Reflection:

Where have you tolerated disorder in the name of freedom? What's one small area—your morning, your eating, your phone usage, your prayers—where you will reestablish discipline starting this week? Name it, set one daily action, and keep it for seven days.

Don't wait for motivation. Start with a decision.

Discipline isn't about becoming impressive. It's about becoming immovable.

X. Reclaiming the Family

Not everyone reading this is a parent. But everyone belongs to a family, comes from one, and shapes one—by what you model, what you tolerate, and what you pass down. The home is the first school of virtue. It is where faith becomes normal, or where confusion becomes tradition. The collapse of the family isn't merely political. It is spiritual and moral. If we want to rebuild the world, we begin where life is formed: at home.

Governments don't raise children. Families do. Homes hand down faith or fog, discipline or disorder, courage or compromise. When homes fracture, culture follows. Fatherlessness wounds the next generation. Masculinity gets mocked or misshaped. Many women are pressured to shrink motherhood and feel guilty for embracing it. Meanwhile children are catechized by screens—trained by algorithms instead of parents. Jordan Peterson is right about the order: the individual, then the family; everything else flows downstream. Deuteronomy gives the method: "These words... you shall teach them diligently to your children... when you sit... when you walk... when you lie down... and when you rise" (Deuteronomy 6:6–7). That's not sentiment. That's strategy.

From my son's first night home, I've aimed to give him the last hour before bed. He's not even a year old, but the rhythm matters. On the rare nights work pulled me away, he took longer to settle and woke again until he saw me in the room. My wife saw it too. So I set a house rule—barring true emergencies, that last hour belongs to him and to his mother. It's a small guardrail with a big purpose: it keeps my duty from drifting.

Practical Guardrails for the Home:

Eat together, screen-free—make the table a sanctuary, not a feed.

Make faith a rhythm: Scripture at night, prayer before meals, truth on walks.

Model what you preach; children copy patterns more than they obey speeches.

Share chores—ownership trains humility and discipline.

Guard the gates: screens, friends, entertainment, and the ideas allowed to live in your house.

Grace is real. Homes can reset. Hard conversations can drain years of resentment; humble acts can restore trust. Firm decisions can reorient a legacy. Not perfection, but presence, courage, and willingness. Strong nations are built on strong homes, and a strong home often begins with a single soul brave enough to change.

A Word to My Son

This isn't only for the world. It's for you. You were not born to inherit confusion, drift in identity, or chase empty love. My job is to build a home where God is honored, righteousness is normal, and your identity is rooted in covenant. If I falter, surpass me—rise earlier, love deeper, walk straighter. Build a home that makes darkness unwelcome and makes generations steady. Renewal starts at the dinner table, in prayer, and in a father's quiet lead. I choose to lead—for you.

Challenge:

Pick one family rhythm—meals, prayer, chores—lacking purpose. Write down one action to strengthen it: a screen-free dinner, a 5-minute prayer, a shared task. Anchor it in Proverbs

22:6. Start today, tell a friend for accountability, and track connection (1–5) after 7 days. Did legacy grow?

XI. The Crossroad: Rebuild or Decay

Every generation faces a crossroad. One path leads to rebuilding what's been weakened—with grit, courage, and clarity. The other leads to decay—masked by comfort, cloaked in distraction, fueled by the lie that someone else will fix it.

The collapse of virtue wasn't sudden. It wasn't one villain or policy. It happened because we allowed it—tolerating what we should have confronted, excusing what we should have confessed, outsourcing what we were called to carry. Schools abandoned truth. Families stopped modeling it. Churches muted it. Culture called it "progress," but it hollowed us out.

Yet a spark remains—you. You're not here by chance. Something in you knows righteousness isn't outdated, masculinity isn't toxic, truth isn't hate speech, and God hasn't given up on this generation. I felt that spark when I refused to nod at a lie in a room that wanted silence. Favor cost me; peace stayed. "For we are His workmanship, created in Christ Jesus for good works, which God prepared beforehand, that we should walk in them." (Ephesians 2:10)

Rebuilding doesn't start with a movement. It starts with a decision—to reject the confusion of the age and become a living blueprint for the next. "Choose this day whom you will serve." (Joshua 24:15) If you won't choose, decay won't stay cultural; it will become personal, generational, eternal.

"You were not made to conform to a broken world. You were made to help restore it."

God is calling you to raise your standards, carry what others drop, speak what others mute, live what others only preach. You don't need permission—you've already been commissioned. History doesn't remember the indifferent. It remembers those who stood when it mattered most.

Challenge:

The One You Wanted to Skip

Look back through every Reflection and Challenge in this chapter. Don't pick the most inspiring one. Pick the one you wanted to skip—the one that exposed you, the one that felt inconvenient.

Write at the top of a page: "This is the one I need."

Then answer, in plain words:

What did it reveal about me?

What would change if I obeyed it for 30 days?

What excuse will try to stop me first?

Now choose one concrete action from that prompt and schedule it today. Make it visible. Make it measurable.

Tell one trusted person: "This is the one I'm obeying," and ask them to check on you weekly until it's done.

Chapter 3

The Mind as Battlefield

I. Every War Begins in the Mind

B efore you compromise with the world, you give ground in thought; before sin takes hold, it tempts in imagination; before you lose your identity, you forget whose you are. The enemy knows this. That's why his first strike is never physical. It's mental. It's subtle. It sounds like this: "What's the point?" "You'll never change." "Everyone else is doing it." "You're too late." "You're too weak." These aren't just insecurities—they are spiritual tactics. And if you don't take them captive, they will take you captive.

Christian-Stoic Principle #1—Control What's Yours; Surrender the Rest

The mind is where this dual calling becomes real: guard what God entrusted to you—and release what God never assigned you to carry. The Stoics framed this with ruthless clarity: distinguish what is "up to you" from what is not. Your judgments, your intentions, your words, your choices—those are yours. Outcomes, timing, the approval of man, the decisions of others, tomorrow itself—those were never yours to command.

But Scripture completes what Stoicism can only outline. The Christian doesn't surrender into fatalism. He surrenders into the care of a Father. "Cast your anxieties on Him, for He cares for you." (1 Peter 5:7). Control what is yours; entrust what isn't.

When you try to manage both, you don't become strong—you become fragmented. But when you discipline your mind and surrender the rest to God, clarity returns.

This is where the battle is won or lost: not in the fact that a thought appears, but in whether you agree with it. A temptation can knock without owning the house. Fear can rise without becoming law. The ancient discipline was to examine impressions before conceding to them—to pause, test, and choose. Scripture calls it by a higher name: the renewing of the mind. "Do not be conformed to this world... be transformed by the renewing of your mind." (Romans 12:2). The mind must be renewed daily, or it drifts toward whatever is loudest.

You can't win a fight you pretend isn't happening. And many men are losing quietly—not because they are evil, but because they are untrained. I was there once. After a work failure, despair settled into my thoughts. It didn't just criticize the moment; it questioned my calling as a father. The fog felt truthful because it felt heavy. But prayer, Psalm 23, and a brother's rebuke cut through it like light through smoke. In that moment I learned something a man can't afford to forget: thoughts are powerful, but they are not sovereign. They must be tested. They must be answered.

Your mind is either your ally or your saboteur. It will either sharpen your convictions or echo the voice of the accuser. And modern noise persuades slowly. The average man today isn't choosing evil with both hands—he's drowning in stimulation, scrolling himself into numbness, letting distraction win battles he never realized he was fighting. The enemy doesn't only tempt through what is vile. He also conquers through what is endless: constant input, fragmented attention, shallow pleasure, low-grade outrage. Noise is often the quietest defeat.

You were not made for that. You were made to guard your thoughts, challenge illusions, and stand watch at the gates of your own mind—because everything else in your life flows from what happens there. If your mind can be steered, your life will be steered. If your mind can be held, your life can be held.

A Word to My Son

You were born into a spiritual war. The world will come for your mind first. I wrote this to help you see the battlefield—so you're not surprised when the fight starts in your thoughts.

When lies rise, answer with truth, not emotion. Stand in God's strength. Like David before Goliath, don't measure the enemy by your size—measure him by the Name you stand under: "I come to you in the name of the LORD of hosts..." (1 Samuel 17:45)

You are not weak. You are not alone.

You were made in the image of God. If you fight well in the mind, the rest becomes winnable—and your legacy of truth will outlive you.

Reflection:

What thought has been circling your mind lately—"I'm too weak," "It's too late," or something else—that you've treated as fact instead of testing it? Write one sentence naming it. Find one Scripture that confronts it (Philippians 4:8 is a strong anchor). Pray that verse for 7 days and take one concrete action in agreement with it. Whatever you tolerate in your thinking will soon dominate your life.

II. Thoughts Become Fortresses

Every repeated thought becomes a belief. Every belief becomes a pattern. And over time, those patterns become a fortress—either a shelter of truth or a stronghold of lies. Repetition is mortar; agreement is cement.

You don't suddenly become enslaved to fear, addiction, or shame. You build it, brick by brick, thought by thought. In darkness, thoughts calcify; in light, they soften and reshape. And unless those thoughts are exposed to the light, they will harden around your soul and define how you see the world, yourself, and God.

"As a man thinks in his heart, so is he." (Proverbs 23:7)

"Man is disturbed not by things, but by the views he takes of them."—Epictetus

The devil doesn't need to destroy you if he can deceive you. Our age industrializes that deception: social feeds and recommendation loops echo "not enough" into a thousand mirrors—body, status, even faith. Billions of micro-agreements train identity before truth can take root. He doesn't always whisper temptation; sometimes he whispers identity:

"You're broken." "You're dirty." "You'll always struggle." "You're just like your father." "You're too far gone." "This is just who you are."

Identity is the doorway; if he wins there, behavior follows.

But God never calls His children by their shame. He calls them by name. He convicts to restore, not to label. And if the enemy can get you to agree with a lie—even quietly—you will build your life on that agreement.

This is the danger of unchecked thought: it becomes structure. And if the structure is corrupt, everything that rests on it eventually collapses. Strongholds aren't events; they're architectures.

That's why Paul tells us to "demolish strongholds" (2 Corinthians 10:4)—not negotiate with them. You don't manage a lie. You destroy it. Peter learned this when fear seized his mind and he denied Christ three times (Luke 22:54–62). Yet after weeping bitterly and meeting the risen Lord, he rebuilt with truth and preached with fire at Pentecost (Acts 2:14–41). His restoration proves lies can be demolished and replaced with God's call to lead.

Name the lie. Renounce the agreement. Replace it with Scripture. Repeat until it becomes reflex. Replace it with truth until it becomes your fortress.

Because here's the reality: You're always building something in your mind. The only question is—what kingdom does your mind serve? Every truth you embrace rebuilds the fortress toward God's kingdom. Start today: replace one lie with His Word and watch clarity return. One renewed mind can shape a legacy that stands—guiding your family, and generations after you, toward righteousness.

"You keep him in perfect peace whose mind is stayed on you, because he trusts in you." (Isaiah 26:3)

Meditation:

The Inner Fortress
Picture your mind as a city with gates. Which gate is unguarded today: fear, lust, resentment, vanity, distraction? Close one gate with a decision, not a fight.
Courage is not loud—it is clean refusal.
Stay until you feel the walls return.

III. The Voices in Your Head

Every man hears voices—not out loud, but deep in his inner world.
Some come from the past, carrying old wounds: "You're not enough." "You always fail."
Others come from culture: "Truth is hate." "Conviction is extremism." "Just do what feels right."
And some come from pressure: deadlines, comparison, expectations you were never meant to carry—all whispering urgency without wisdom.

Social feeds amplify these competing signals, training your instincts and drowning out the quiet things that matter.

And then there's the voice of God—still, steady, often lost beneath the noise.

Most men never learn how to sort the voices. So they follow whichever one is loudest, or whichever one feels safest in the moment. That voice becomes their compass—not because it's true, but because it's familiar.

If you don't train your mind to recognize the voice of God, you'll obey the voice of fear, impulse, ego, or pressure. Elijah learned this after fleeing Jezebel: God was not in the wind, earthquake, or fire, but in a low whisper (1 Kings 19:11–13). When the noise quieted, clarity returned.

Over time, the voices you entertain will begin to sound like your own thoughts—until you can't tell where the lie ends and you begin.

"No man is free who is not master of his thoughts."—Marcus Aurelius

Silence matters—not to escape voices, but to expose them. You don't need more content—you need more clarity. You need stillness. Reflection. Time to test the voices that shape your decisions.

Because not every voice deserves authority. Not every thought deserves to be entertained. And not every feeling comes from your Father.

You will hear many voices in this life—some from people you trust, some from wounds you don't expect, and some from within.

When that happens, I want you to know something:
You are not crazy. You are not broken. You are not alone.
But you must learn to listen for the right voice.

God is not the loudest—but He is always the clearest.
He does not flatter, but He never condemns.
He will correct you—but always with love, always with purpose.

If you hear a voice that tries to shame you without offering a way forward—that's not your Father. That's the accuser. Silence him. Open your Bible. Remember who you are, and build a legacy of hearing God's truth.

Reflection:

Whose voice do you trust most—culture, fear, or God? Take 10 minutes in silence today—no phone, no noise, just a pen and one verse (e.g., John 10:27). Ask God to speak, write what you hear, and repeat for 7 days. Track clarity each day (1–5). Did His voice grow clearer? Note one behavioral shift (e.g., less distraction).

IV. Hijacked by Design

Your mind was not made for constant intrusion. It was made for clarity, reflection, and truth. But in today's world, your thoughts are not simply distracted—they are hijacked.

Platforms don't inform—they addict; they don't strengthen—they manipulate. You are not the customer—you are the product. And your attention is the currency.

Modern minds are trained by repetition, not wisdom. What you see, you begin to absorb. What you absorb, you begin to believe. And soon, your worldview is not shaped by truth—but by trending content.

Algorithms are not neutral. They're designed to reward the flesh: impulse, ego, lust, rage, vanity. Not because they're evil in themselves—but because they were built for profit, not purity.

That's what makes this war so subtle. You don't feel attacked—you feel entertained. But your mind, slowly, becomes less capable of silence, less willing to resist, and more dependent on stimulation.

"Where your treasure is, there your heart will be also."—Jesus (Matthew 6:21)

Attention is the treasury of the heart; in the Sermon on the Mount, Jesus directs that treasury toward God's kingdom, not the feed.

So where is your attention? Where is your energy? Where is your identity being shaped—by God's Word or by a curated feed designed to keep you addicted?

"A man's worth is no greater than the worth of his ambitions."—Marcus Aurelius

What happens when your ambitions have been fed to you by a machine?

What happens when the deepest parts of you are shaped by something you didn't choose—but never questioned?

This isn't paranoia. It's pattern recognition. And if you want to win the war for your mind, you must unplug long enough to remember who you are—and whose you are, rebuilding clarity that leaves a legacy of truth for your family.

Because the longer you stay hijacked, the more the truth sounds like static.

Challenge:

Identify one app or feed that hijacks your attention most (e.g., short-video apps, infinite news/social feeds). Remove it for 7 days. Each day, replace that slot with Scripture (e.g., Matthew 6:21), journaling, or deliberate stillness. Track your clarity (1–5) daily. Did peace grow? Let your silence speak louder than the noise.

V. Anxiety, Fear, and the Fog of War

In combat, soldiers speak of "the fog"—the mental cloud of adrenaline, confusion, and chaos that makes even the strongest hesitate. But you don't need to be on a battlefield to feel it. Most people today live in that fog—not from bullets or bombs, but from anxiety, fear, and spiritual noise.
You can see it in their eyes: distracted, fragile, unsure.
You hear it in their words: "I feel overwhelmed." "I don't know who I am." "I just want peace."
And you've likely felt it yourself—the racing thoughts, the tight chest, the constant hum of unrest in the background of your life.

A hard truth: fear left unchecked becomes your reality—not because it's true, but because you built a world around it.

Anxiety isn't just a feeling—it's a filter that distorts silence, criticism, delay, or uncertainty, becoming the lens for your identity, relationships, and faith if unchallenged.
The Stoics understood this well. Epictetus warned that most suffering begins when we try to control what's outside our control. That insight still rings true.

But modern life pulls the mind in every direction. When your peace depends on outcomes, opinions, or algorithms, you'll always feel one moment away from collapse. And if you're not grounded, fear becomes your default operating system.

If you believe you're alone... If you believe your past defines you... If you believe your failure is final... You're not just anxious—you're under attack. Fear exploits unbelief and erode righteousness, shifting allegiance from God's unchanging promises to fragile self-control.

The fog grows thick when truth is absent. And in that fog, the mind loses clarity—the soul becomes reactive, not reflective.

"The Lord is my light and my salvation—whom shall I fear?" (Psalm 27:1)

David knew that fog while pursued by Saul—hunted and outnumbered—yet he declared God's light pierced the chaos; surrender, not sheer strength, led him through.

You don't need to feel strong to move forward. You just need to know what light to follow. And that light isn't found in more noise, more scrolling, or more self-affirmation. It's found in truth. In stillness. In surrender.

Fear isn't conquered by pretending it's not there. It's conquered when you choose to walk through the fog, eyes fixed on what's unchanging.

Peace doesn't come from knowing what's ahead. It comes from knowing who's with you—right now.

Prayer:

Lord, I bring You the fear I keep rehearsing. I refuse to be ruled by imagined outcomes. Give me courage to do the next right thing, not a craving for certainty. Train my thoughts to obey truth, not threat. If I must walk through a storm, keep my feet on the path. Amen.

VI. Rebuilding Mental Discipline

A broken mind cannot lead a strong life. We live in a time where physical fitness is celebrated—but mental discipline is ignored. People track steps, measure macros, and follow strict routines for their bodies... yet let their thoughts roam unchecked. They feed every emotion, obey every impulse, and allow distraction to lead the day. You can't have peace without structure. You can't have clarity without control. You can't have wisdom without training.

Christian–Stoic Principle #4—Master Desires and Impulses; Renew the Mind

The Stoics taught that mastery begins with ruling the inner world—disciplining desire, quieting impulse, and training attention. They focused on what happens between the stimulus and the response: the moment an impression hits, before you agree with it. If you learn to pause, examine, and choose, you stop living as a slave to appetite. You become governed.

The ancients didn't treat discipline as punishment—they treated it as freedom. Marcus Aurelius trained his mind daily through reflection and self-correction. Epictetus taught that people are not disturbed by events, but by the judgments they place on events. The battle is not first "out there." It's in the mind's consent. These weren't abstractions; they were conditioning—daily practice that formed a man's character.

Scripture completes what the philosophers could only reach toward. The believer is not called merely to manage impulses, but to renew the mind itself (Romans 12:2). Mastery is not repression; it is reorientation—ordering the mind under God so that desires bend to truth, rather than truth bending to desire. Discipline isn't mere willpower; it's alignment—a trained mind, steady enough to think clearly and strong enough to stand firm.

Mental discipline means learning to pause before reacting. It means rejecting the lie that emotion should always be obeyed. Feelings are information, not commandments. The disciplined man can feel deeply and still act wisely, be angry and refuse vengeance. He can be afraid and still do what's right, be tempted and still stay clean. He chooses order when the world celebrates chaos—and he directs his thoughts instead of being dragged by noise.

In a culture that rewards impulsiveness, a disciplined mind is a rare weapon. It filters lies, blocks manipulation, and protects conscience. It turns down the volume of the crowd so you can hear the voice of truth.

This is also maturity. Paul modeled it from prison—rooted in purpose, writing hope-filled epistles under chains. His circumstances didn't possess him, because Christ possessed him. Discipline doesn't make you robotic—it makes you rooted.

And yes, you'll slip. Everyone does. But a disciplined mind doesn't stay down. It repents, resets, rebuilds, and refocuses—because it remembers the mission.

Meditation:

Morning Reset
Before the day claims you, claim your stance.
Breathe. Choose one sentence to govern your next hours:
"I will act with wisdom, justice, courage, and temperance."
Repeat it slowly until it becomes posture, not poetry.

VII. The Lies We Believe

Every broken life begins with a lie—not always loud, but always repeated.

"You're not good enough." "You'll always be this way." "No one will love the real you." "Truth is whatever you feel." "God is disappointed in you."

These don't just live in the mind—they burrow into identity. Over time, they shape how you see yourself, how you treat others, how you relate to God. Most dangerously, they begin to feel like truth.

"The soul becomes dyed with the color of its thoughts."—Marcus Aurelius

The Stoics taught us to question impressions and examine the logic behind emotions. But Christianity goes deeper—it doesn't just ask you to evaluate thoughts. It asks you to surrender them.

"Take every thought captive to make it obedient to Christ." —2 Corinthians 10:5

That command isn't poetic. It's surgical. Because not every belief you hold is true—and not every feeling you trust is honest.

Some lies were planted in childhood. Others came through trauma. Still others crept in through culture, media, or sin. And none of them have to stay. Corrie ten Boom lived this: imprisoned by the Nazis and bereaved, she confronted the lies of hatred and worthlessness; anchored in Psalm 28:7 ("The Lord is my strength and my shield"), she forgave her captors and preached Christ—proof that truth breaks the strongest chains.

The devil rarely tempts with rebellion. He tempts with imitation—with half-truths dressed as compassion, and slogans that sound like freedom but end in slavery.

"Live your truth. Follow your heart. Be true to yourself."

These may feel empowering, but often, they're just prettier chains. Because if your truth contradicts God's, it's not freedom, it's deception.

"You're not on a truth quest—you're on a happiness quest. And you'll believe whatever makes you feel happy... until it breaks you."—attributed to Dr. Frank Turek. Echoing Matthew 4, where Satan twisted Scripture to imitate truth. Imitation lures; only God's Word liberates.

True freedom doesn't come from doing whatever you want. It comes from knowing what's right—and aligning your life with it.

You are not your trauma. You are not your temptation. You are not your failures. You are not your feelings.

You are who God says you are.

And when that becomes your foundation, the lies begin to lose their power.

Even so—they will try to come back. They'll whisper when you're tired. They'll disguise themselves as your own voice. That's why discernment matters. That's why Scripture matters. That's why silence matters.

Because in silence, you can hear what's been hiding. And in truth, you can confront it.

Reflection:

What lie have you accepted about yourself—something you would never say to someone you love, but you quietly believe about you? Choose one verse that contradicts the lie; speak it morning and night for 7 days. Replace it. Track your peace (1–5) and note one action you took in agreement with truth. Repeat it daily until the lie fades—reclaiming your mind verse by verse.

VIII. Guarding the Gate

Your mind has a gate—and you are the gatekeeper.

Most people would never leave their home unlocked. They protect their passwords, guard their finances, and set boundaries around their children. But when it comes to their thoughts, they leave the door wide open. And the enemy doesn't need your approval—only your attention.

Guarding your mind doesn't mean becoming paranoid or rigid. It means becoming intentional—deciding what enters by asking: Who gets a voice in my thoughts? What content claims my time? What values are shaping my inner life? The Stoics practiced this through daily self-examination. Marcus Aurelius would journal at night, questioning his motives, pruning his desires. But Christianity adds more than discipline—it adds divine alignment.

"Above all else, guard your heart, for everything you do flows from it." (Proverbs 4:23)

Guarding the gate starts with setting standards:

What kind of media do you allow into your mind?

Who do you listen to—and why?

Are your daily influences aligned with righteousness, or just popular?

But it's not just defense—it's nourishment. I practiced this in a season of intentional singleness: I barred anything that fed lust from my gate and filled the quiet with Scripture and prayer. The cravings didn't vanish overnight—but guardrails plus God's Word turned noise into clarity, and clarity into peace (Philippians 4:8). You can't only say no to the bad; you must say yes to what builds. Nehemiah's men rebuilt with a trowel in one hand and a sword in the other (Nehemiah 4): watch and work, guard and grow. "Whatever is true, whatever is noble, whatever is right... think about such things." (Philippians 4:8)

Your mind is a fortress under pressure. If the walls are weak, the world gets in. If the walls are strong, the truth stays protected. And when lies try to sneak through—because they will—you'll know how to answer: not with panic, but with peace; not with emotion alone, but with discernment.

Protect the gate. And feed the fortress.

Challenge:

For the next 3 days, ask these three questions before you consume anything—media, advice, ideas: Does this lead me toward truth—or confusion? Does this strengthen my faith—or weaken it? Would I allow this if Christ were sitting next to me? Note one rejection daily and rate your clarity (1–5). You are not a victim of your thoughts. You are their protector.

IX. The Armor of Truth

In every age, people build defenses—some out of pride, others out of pain. But most don't realize that their greatest protection isn't what they project—it's what they believe.

Truth is armor. And in a world that rewards conformity over conviction, that armor has never been more essential.

Today, truth is not just debated—it's distorted. Wrapped in feelings. Softened for comfort. Shaped to fit convenience. And once truth loses its sharpness, righteousness becomes impossible.

This is why Paul told the church in Ephesus to put on the full armor of God—and the first piece he named was truth.

"Stand firm then, with the belt of truth buckled around your waist…" (Ephesians 6:14)

"The sum of your word is truth" (Psalm 119:160). Truth doesn't fray, it binds every piece in steady integrity.

A soldier without a belt couldn't carry his weapons. Nothing stayed in place. Truth holds everything together.

But truth isn't just a concept. It's a Person. "I am the way and the truth and the life."—Jesus (John 14:6)

"The word of God is living and active, sharper than any two-edged sword" (Hebrews 4:12); truth doesn't sit still—it cuts, discerns, and defends.

If Christ is truth, then truth is not up for debate. It doesn't shift with opinion polls. It doesn't evolve to fit comfort. It simply is and it divides—clarity from confusion, wisdom from impulse, conviction from performance.

Epictetus urged us to test impressions for truth; Scripture grounds that testing as our moral compass: "Sanctify them in the truth; your word is truth" (John 17:17). Divine discernment, not fleeting happiness, forges clarity.

But here's the paradox: truth isn't always comfortable, but it's always freeing.

It's the armor that keeps you from being owned by lies. It's the lens that makes sense of chaos. It's the weight that keeps you grounded when culture tries to lift you into confusion.

And it must be worn daily—not just believed intellectually, but embodied practically.

You don't "put on" truth with a quote or a tweet. You put it on by living it when it's inconvenient. By speaking it when it costs you. By obeying it when no one else does.

That's when it becomes armor—not just language.

"Therefore take up the whole armor of God, that you may be able to withstand in the evil day..." (Ephesians 6:13)
And the day is evil. Not in theory—in reality.
Confusion is marketed as kindness. Cowardice is praised as tolerance. Sin is relabeled as freedom. And those who stand for truth are called dangerous.
But danger is not found in those who speak truth—it's found in those who abandon it.
   You are not called to be liked. You are called to be equipped. And truth is your first line of defense—not because it protects your reputation, but because it protects your soul.

Challenge:

Memorize Ephesians 6:10–18 this week—not just for knowledge, but for strength. Then, identify one recent lie you've seen in your feed, your circle, or your own thoughts. Write it down—and confront it with Scripture. Apply that Scripture in one concrete decision today, and note how truth divides confusion from conviction. Don't just admire the armor—wear it daily, verse by verse, until lies shatter and righteousness stands unshaken.

X. Mastery of the Inner War

There is no greater battle than the one no one sees.
Not fought in crowds or protests. Not broadcast online. It happens in silence—in your thought life, your habits, your impulses, and your identity.
It's the war within.
   Every soul feels it: the tension between who you are and who you could be. Between discipline and distraction. Truth and temptation. Conviction and comfort.
   The Stoics knew this war well. Marcus Aurelius wrestled with ego, loss, and control. Seneca wrote about mastering desire and preparing for death with clarity. But their tools—reason,

reflection, restraint—could only go so far.

Because the war isn't just philosophical. It's spiritual.

"The mind governed by the flesh is death, but the mind governed by the Spirit is life and peace." (Romans 8:6)

You are not just fighting feelings—you are fighting forces. The flesh resists discipline. The world rewards compromise. And the enemy whispers in moments of weakness.

But here's the truth:

You were never meant to fight alone. And you were not designed to surrender.

"Those who belong to Christ Jesus have crucified the flesh with its passions and desires." (Galatians 5:24)

Seneca pursued mastery by rational restraint; Scripture lifts it higher: "I count everything as loss because of the surpassing worth of knowing Christ" (Philippians 3:8). True mastery comes as surrender to Him crucifies the flesh.

The path to mastery is not the pursuit of perfection. It's the pursuit of preparation.

It's waking up and deciding: I will lead my mind before it leads me. I will bring my thoughts under obedience. I will train my will to follow what is right—not what is easy.

He who conquers himself is the mightiest warrior.

And in Christ, self-mastery becomes Spirit-led mastery.

But let's be honest: there will be days when the war inside you feels louder than your prayers. When temptation doesn't just knock—it breaks in. When shame returns. When doubt creeps. When quitting seems like peace.

Don't surrender—remember you were made for this fight, designed to win it not by willpower alone, but by aligning with the Overcomer.

"In this world you will have trouble. But take heart! I have overcome the world."—Jesus (John 16:33)

"Thanks be to God, who gives us the victory through our Lord Jesus Christ" (1 Corinthians 15:57).

Even the strongest men fall. But the ones who master the inner war rise again—not because they never wavered, but because they refused to stay down.

They trained their mind. They ruled their emotions. They didn't chase peace through silence; they found it by surrendering to truth.

And when the flesh rose, they remembered who they were—and whose they were.

You don't need to be fearless to fight. You just need to show up. Again. And again. And again.

Because the devil doesn't fear your talent. He fears your endurance.

Challenge:

What part of your inner life still leads you instead of being led—lust, ego, fear, addiction, comparison, comfort? Name it. Confront it. Then build one new habit this week that strengthens your spirit over your flesh and memorize Romans 8:6—declare it daily. Note one victory this week, tracking how the Spirit strengthens your compass. The final enemy isn't out there. It's in here. And through Christ—it can be mastered.

Chapter 4

What Is Righteousness?

I. The Standard Beyond Morality

M orality changes with culture. Righteousness does not. What is considered good in one generation may be mocked in the next. Laws shift. Values drift. But righteousness—the standard of what is right before God—stays fixed, not because man enforces it, but because God defines it.

A man can look moral and still be unrighteous. He can match the spirit of his age and still miss eternity. That's the trap of relativism: virtue that bends to applause, not truth.

Righteousness isn't about being better than others. It's about aligning with truth—whatever the price.

This is what separated the prophets from the politicians, the disciples from the crowd. They didn't ask, "What's acceptable?" They asked, "What's holy?" On Mount Carmel (1 Kings 18), Elijah faced fashionable gods with unshakable obedience. Baal answered with silence; the Lord answered with fire. Righteousness doesn't come from consensus. It comes from covenant. Even the Stoics glimpsed this principle: the good remains good even when the crowd refuses to praise it. Righteousness aims at God, not approval.

"Blessed are those who hunger and thirst for righteousness, for they shall be filled."—Jesus (Matthew 5:6).

To hunger for righteousness is to long for a life aligned with God—not just in behavior, but in thought, desire, and purpose. It's not self-righteousness. It's surrendered righteousness.

You don't earn it. You seek it. And when you do, you begin to see the difference between performance and purity, between popularity and holiness, between being liked and being right with God.

"Seek first the kingdom of God and His righteousness…" (Matthew 6:33)

The world will keep redefining morality. But you were not called to keep up with the world. You were called to align with the One who never changes.

Reflection:

This week, ask God to deepen your hunger for His righteousness—because hunger for Him ends in fullness, not in approval. Name one place you've chosen "acceptable" over "holy," and take a single step that realigns you with what satisfies forever.

II. Righteousness Across Cultures

Every civilization has a code—a way of separating good from evil, noble from disgraceful, just from corrupt. These codes differ in form but share a surprising pattern: they reach beyond man to a higher measure.

In ancient Greece, Socrates was executed for challenging the moral corruption of his city—not with violence, but with virtue. In ancient China, Confucian ethics taught that righteousness must come before profit. In early Israel, righteousness was so central that kings were judged not by power, but by whether they did "what was right in the eyes of the Lord."

Even cultures that didn't know the God of Scripture still reached for moral order. Paul alludes to this in Romans 2:15, when he says that the law is "written on their hearts." Something deep within humanity yearns to be right with whatever power or truth governs reality. But admiration is not submission.

Epictetus warned that opinion often masquerades as goodness unless tested against a higher rule; what looks noble in public can evaporate in the dark unless it's rooted in something higher than human approval.

Modern culture loves to borrow from righteous principles—justice, compassion, dignity—but often divorces them from their Source. It wants the fruit without the root; cut from the root, the fruit rots into slogans.

"Woe to those who call evil good and good evil, who put darkness for light and light for darkness." (Isaiah 5:20)

The result? Tolerance that silences truth, virtue-talk that hides vice, systems that weaponize "righteousness" for unrighteous ends.

But God is not fooled by cultural packaging. He sees the heart. Righteousness cannot be crowdsourced; it must be revealed.

That's why it's not enough to "do what feels right" or follow the crowd. Righteousness isn't based on majority opinion. It's based on God's eternal nature.

"All his laws are before me; I have not turned away from his decrees." (2 Samuel 22:23)

The world changes. Nations rise and fall. God's standard does not. Our task is not to update it, but to align with it.

Reflection:

Which cultural values shape your sense of "right," and what is their root?

Test them against God's revealed truth—then trade admiration for obedience in one concrete step this week.

You were made for more than cultural virtue. You were made for righteousness.

III. The Mirror of the Law

Righteousness isn't discovered by comparing ourselves to others. It's revealed when we compare ourselves to the law of God—and realize how far short we fall.

The law is not a ladder to climb. It's a mirror. And when you stand in front of it with honesty, it doesn't flatter you. It exposes you. Not to shame, but to awaken.

"Through the law we become conscious of sin." (Romans 3:20)

The modern world doesn't like this idea. It wants grace without truth. Love without standards. Progress without repentance.

But you can't seek righteousness unless you first admit unrighteousness. You can't appreciate grace unless you first see your need for it. That's why the law is a gift. It tells the truth about us—so we stop pretending and start repenting. This is why the great reformers spoke of the law as a mirror: it exposes sin to drive us to Christ, not to leave us in despair.

Jesus didn't come to erase the law. He came to fulfill it—and to offer Himself as the only One who kept it perfectly.

"Do not think that I have come to abolish the Law or the Prophets; I have not come to abolish them but to fulfill them." (Matthew 5:17)

This is what separates Christianity from man-made religion: every other system says "do more, be better, try harder," while the gospel says, "you can't—but Christ did."

The mirror of the law doesn't leave you stuck in guilt. It points you to the only One who is righteous—and then invites you to follow Him, not in perfection, but in pursuit.

"For Christ is the end of the law for righteousness to everyone who believes." (Romans 10:4)

You don't fix the mirror when you don't like what it shows. You let it show you the truth. Then you go to the only One who can make you new.

Prayer:

God, search me and tell me the truth about me. I confess the sin I have renamed, the obedience I have delayed, and the pride I have protected. Do not let me perform righteousness while my heart stays unchanged. Forgive me, cleanse me, and strengthen me to obey at a cost. Make me whole. Amen.

IV. The Imitation Trap

Imitation is cheap when appearance is everything and depth is optional.

People know how to look righteous without being righteous. They curate their image, master the language, and surround themselves with people who validate their virtue. But imitation isn't transformation.

It's easy to copy convictions without counting their cost, mimic character unseen, or look holy on camera. Plato pictured this in the Ring of Gyges: give a man invisibility and watch "virtue" collapse when there's no audience; the ring exposes how appearances can masquerade as justice. Epictetus pressed the opposite path: "A good man does nothing for appearance's sake, but for the sake of having done right," pointing to hope in a righteousness forged beyond visibility, not performance.

"Be careful not to practice your righteousness in front of others to be seen by them..."—Jesus (Matthew 6:1).

Righteousness is not performance. It's posture. And the moment you start performing for the crowd, you've already left the presence of God.

This is what Jesus confronted in the Pharisees—not because they followed the law, but because they used it as a mask. They wanted praise more than purity. Applause more than alignment. And this isn't new: when Samuel saw Eliab, he was sure the tallest, most impressive son must be God's choice—but the Lord rejected the spectacle and chose David, the overlooked shepherd. God reminded His prophet that He weighs the hidden heart, not the polished exterior (1 Samuel 16:7). That same divine discernment still forges true righteousness beyond masks.

"Woe to you... You are like whitewashed tombs, which look beautiful on the outside but on the inside are full of bones..."—Jesus (Matthew 23:27)

This same spirit exists today. You see it in churches that look trendy but preach compromise. In leaders who speak of virtue but live in shadows. In men who wear crosses but don't carry them.

But true righteousness can't be faked. It's refined in private. It's forged through obedience. It flows from intimacy with God—not the opinions of men.

"The LORD sees not as man sees: man looks on the outward appearance, but the LORD looks on the heart." (1 Samuel 16:7)

You don't need to look righteous. You need to be righteous. And that begins when you stop imitating others—and start walking with the One who made you.

Reflection:

Where have you been tempted to imitate righteousness instead of pursue it? Ask God to reveal where performance has replaced pursuit, then return with honesty—anchored in heart-level obedience that endures beyond applause and forges eternal depth.

V. When Good isn't Godly

Modern culture is full of causes that look righteous, sound compassionate, and carry the language of justice—yet produce the opposite fruit. Slogans can imitate virtue. Movements can borrow God's vocabulary while rejecting God's order. When the root is rebellion, the outcome will not be healing; it will be confusion dressed as liberation.

"Modern feminism" is one of the clearest examples. Its earliest aims—legal protection, civic dignity, equal regard before the law—fit with justice. That is not the issue. The issue is the drift in many modern streams: dignity gets replaced with domination, complement becomes conflict, and womanhood is treated as a costume instead of a created reality. When male-bodied competitors are welcomed into women's sports and honors, and that erasure is praised as virtue, the movement is no longer protecting women. It is redefining them out of existence.

Strength is not found in rebellion. It is found in harmony with design.

"A wife of noble character who can find? She is worth far more than rubies." (Proverbs 31:10)

Proverbs 31 doesn't diminish a woman; it crowns her. She builds, trades, plans, serves, and strengthens her arms—wisdom with steel in it. Her strength grows from truth, not trends; from faithfulness, not performance.

A Word to My Son

You'll hear many voices defining "strong." Measure them by fruit. Look for a woman who honors God, loves without theatrics, speaks life, and builds what lasts. Choose a wife who shares your convictions and values righteousness over reputation. Then be the kind of man worthy of her trust.

True righteousness isn't found in a hashtag or a revolt. It's found at the Cross. And anything that pulls you away from Christ—no matter how moral it sounds—cannot lead you into life.

"When a movement demands that reality bend to desire, it stops protecting the vulnerable and starts sacrificing them."

Challenge:

What beliefs or causes have you supported that seemed good—but produced confusion, bitterness, or pride?
Don't just check the message. Check the fruit.
If it doesn't lead toward Christ's righteousness—leave it behind.
Strip away the image and ask: what would your faith look like if no one could see it?
God doesn't need actors. He needs vessels.

VI. Anchored, Not Performed

Applause is loud. Truth is quiet. And only one of them can anchor your soul.

True righteousness is never about being seen. It's about being anchored.

We live in a culture obsessed with metrics, validation, and visibility, but the soul was not designed to live from public opinion, only from private alignment.

The Pharisees did everything right on the outside. But their hearts were far from God. Their prayers were loud, but hollow. Their rituals were polished, but prideful.

Jesus never said they lacked effort. He said they lacked depth. In Matthew 23 Jesus exposed religion-as-performance, leaders who did the right things for the wrong audience. He called them back to obedience that could stand before God when the crowd was gone. That is the hope: righteousness that survives divine scrutiny because it is real, not rehearsed.

"They honor me with their lips, but their hearts are far from me." (Matthew 15:8)

You can obey all the rules and still be lost. You can impress the crowd and still grieve the Spirit. You can look like a light and still walk in darkness.

Because righteousness is not reputation. It's alignment.

Psychologically, we crave affirmation. But spiritually, we were made for truth. That's why many people burn out—they perform goodness, but never internalize it.

Being anchored means walking in truth when no one is watching. It means honoring your convictions in silence, when there's no spotlight to reward you.

"We have this hope as an anchor for the soul, firm and secure." (Hebrews 6:19)

An anchored man doesn't need applause. He doesn't need performance. He doesn't need to prove anything. His foundation is firm—not because he's perfect, but because he's planted.

"Waste no more time arguing what a good man should be. Be one."—Marcus Aurelius (Meditations 10.16).

In the Meditations he pushes action over display—virtue as alignment with rational nature (logos)—a Stoic insistence on being rather than arguing, which pairs with the gospel's quiet truth to steady the soul.

And when the winds come—because they will—he won't move.

Meditation:

Sit as if no one will ever praise you. Notice how often you rehearse being seen.

Release the performance. Justice begins when you do what is right without applause.

Hold still until integrity feels heavier than image.

VII. The Weight of Grace

Grace is beautiful—but it's not light.
When you truly understand grace, it humbles you. It breaks you. It strips away the illusion that you earned your place before God.

The modern world turns grace into sentiment—a soft word, a permission slip, a feel-good fallback—but that isn't grace; it's indulgence dressed in mercy's clothes.
Real grace doesn't excuse sin. It pays for it. With blood. With sweat. With a cross.

"For you were bought at a price. Therefore glorify God in your body and in your spirit, which are God's." (1 Corinthians 6:20)

Grace is not cheap. It cost Jesus everything. As Thomas Aquinas framed it: grace does not destroy nature but perfects it—redeeming our weakness into worshipful obedience. And when you receive it rightly, you don't walk away proud. You walk away stunned.

You don't abuse grace when you understand the weight of it. You respond to it with obedience. With worship. With the quiet resolve to live a life worthy of the gift.

"Shall we go on sinning so that grace may increase? By no means!" (Romans 6:1–2)
Paul presses the image: in baptism we were buried with Christ—the old self laid in the ground—and raised so we might walk in newness of life. Grace becomes mastery, not a loophole; the tyrant of sin is dethroned, and a humbled obedience rises from the water. Hope lives here: grace's weight empowers a steady walk without arrogance or indulgence.

There's a reason righteous men don't flaunt their good-ness—they know what it cost to be redeemed. And they know they didn't pay for it.
Grace doesn't create arrogance. It destroys it.
It reminds you that righteousness isn't about climbing to heav-

en. It's about heaven coming down to rescue you when you had nothing left to offer.

That's why the man who walks in grace walks with a limp. He knows what he was. He knows what he's been given. And he knows Who gave it.

Reflection:

When you think about grace, do you feel light—or its cost's weight? Thank God in five minutes' silence, letting it settle; then carry it with honor, fueling a humbled pursuit of worthy, eternal living.

VIII. The Fruit of Obedience

Obedience isn't glamorous. It doesn't get applause. It rarely feels powerful. But it's the soil where righteousness grows.

In a world obsessed with expression, obedience can feel restrictive—people want to follow their hearts, not submit them; to feel righteous, not become it—but Jesus never said, "If you feel like it, follow Me." He said, "If you love Me, obey My commandments."

"If you love Me, keep My commandments." (John 14:15)

The fruit of obedience is not immediate. It's cultivated over time. You may not see the reward right away, but something is being built—deep roots, clean hands, a steady heart.

Obedience sharpens your discernment. It protects your peace. It exposes lies you didn't even know you believed. And eventually, it bears fruit—not just in your life, but in those around you. Noah obeyed when it made no sense to his generation; for decades—traditionally told as up to 120 years, though the textual timeline places construction under a century—he worked an ark under open mockery. His unseen obedience became shelter when the waters rose, and God sealed it with a covenant: reward delayed, conviction rooted. When obedience seems to bury rather than promote, remember Joseph:

betrayed, sold, and forgotten, he kept faith in Potiphar's house and in prison, honoring God where no one applauded, until God raised him to spare multitudes in famine. Then look to the summit—Jesus obeyed to the end, and by that obedience redeemed the world.

"Although He was a Son, He learned obedience from the things which He suffered." (Hebrews 5:8)

Suffering often accompanies obedience. It costs you friends. It invites mockery. It may isolate you. But what you gain in return is infinitely greater: the favor of God, the clarity of conscience, the strength of conviction.

History bears the same pattern: consider William Wilberforce (1759–1833). Decades of steady, costly obedience in Parliament helped end the British slave trade in 1807 and brought about the abolition of slavery across the Empire in 1833—habitual submission yielding generational freedom and societal transformation, showing how obedience's quiet persistence can shake empires and echo into eternity.

And that's the kind of fruit this world can't produce.

You don't obey to earn righteousness—you obey because righteousness has taken root in you. You obey because you know who your Father is. And when the path is narrow, you trust the Gardener.

"Blessed are those who hear the word of God and obey it." (Luke 11:28)

Obedience may look quiet. But its fruit shakes eternity.

Reflection:

When was the last time you obeyed God at a cost? Identify delayed obedience—what fruit has that delay produced? Choose obedience—not ease, but rightness—rooting your life in divine cultivation that bears eternal weight.

IX. The Righteous Legacy

Your legacy is not built in the spotlight. It's built in secret—in your choices, your habits, your convictions, and the people you love most.

Righteousness is not just a gift. It's a seed. And every day you water it, it grows into something your children can stand on.

You may never be known by the world. But if your son learns to love truth, if your daughter walks in wisdom, if your family walks in peace—then you've won.

The righteous don't just make noise. They make impact. They lay roots.

"The righteous man walks in his integrity; his children are blessed after him." (Proverbs 20:7)

Integrity is a path, not a pose—a straight way cut through the brambles of appetite and applause that plants what your children can walk on when the world pulls them sideways. Unseen choices today become shelter tomorrow—a quiet root system of favor that outlives the man who planted it.

One day, your son or your grandson will face a fork in the road. He'll feel the pull of the world, the temptation to drift. He won't need a lecture. He'll need a memory. Of a man who stood firm. Who lived clean. Who didn't compromise.

That memory won't come from your speeches. It will come from your example.

Legacy isn't declared. It's demonstrated. And the proof is how you live when no one's watching. When your life proves true, its echo carries—from household to church, to street, to city—leaving a trail of righteousness that ripples outward under divine favor and into eternity.

To my readers—build something better. Walk in truth; be faithful; speak boldly; honor your mother and father; protect the weak; keep your word; and when you fall, rise again with humility and fire.

Your righteousness will never be perfect. But it will be visible. It will be felt. And it will echo beyond your life.

"A good man leaves an inheritance to his children's children..." (Proverbs 13:22)

Let that inheritance begin now—not with money, but with righteousness. Not with assets, but with honor. That is a legacy worth leaving.

Challenge:

Write three traits you want in the next generation. Ask: do they show up in me today? Legacy is lived now, not later—rooted in righteousness that carries forward through divine inheritance and multigenerational roots.

Chapter 5

Truth Is Not Relative

I. The Foundation of Reality

Truth is not a matter of opinion. It isn't shaped by feelings, popular vote, or the shifting winds of culture. Reality is what is—no matter who believes it, and no matter how it makes you feel.

"Truth is like a lion. You don't have to defend it. Let it loose. It will defend itself."—attributed to Augustine

This is the foundation of reality: truth exists outside of you. It doesn't rise from within. It doesn't adapt to your identity. You conform to it—or you live in deception.

We live in an age obsessed with perception, where children are taught that truth is personal, adults are told it's oppressive, and entire systems—education, media, politics—treat facts as flexible illusions serving emotion and power.

But truth doesn't care if you're offended. It only cares if you're aligned.

"Sanctify them by the truth; your word is truth."—Jesus (John 17:17)

This doesn't present truth as a human invention. It declares a standard that judges us. And if God's Word is truth, then reality is not merely abstract—it is anchored in Someone higher than culture.

When Thomas struggled to grasp the road ahead, he asked how anyone could know the way. Jesus didn't hand him a theory. He pointed to Himself. In that moment, truth wasn't a concept—it was a Person. Direction was no longer an idea to debate, but a relationship to follow.

When you disconnect truth from God, you get what we have now: Identity confusion labeled as progress. Spiritual apathy masked as tolerance. Cultural lies marketed as kindness.

But all of it rests on sand. Remove the standard, and justice collapses. Remove the anchor, and morality drifts. Remove the compass, and people lose the path.

If you remove truth from virtue, you do not get compassion—you get chaos.

As believers, we aren't searching for something to stand on—we're anchored. Our confidence isn't a concept; it's a Person, crucified and risen. Unchanged. Unmoving. Unbreakable.

In a world that tells you to craft your own version of reality, stand on the One who speaks reality into being.

Reflection:

What part of your life has been shaped more by emotion than by truth? Where have you adjusted God's Word to fit your desires—rather than adjusting your desires to fit His Word? Align now. Hope isn't found in redefining reality, but in surrendering to the One who is it.

II. The Death of Objective Truth

Truth did not vanish—it was traded. Not for wisdom or agreement, but for control. The modern world did not abandon reason by mistake; it rejected it on purpose. Because the moment reality exists outside of you, it limits your power to reshape the world in your image.

So reality was put on trial. Mocked in universities that treat clarity like oppression. Diluted in media that profits from confusion. Weaponized by politicians who need chaos to maintain power. And quietly buried by citizens more fearful of disapproval than dishonesty.

The verdict was simple: silence what is real so the self can stay sovereign.

"When men choose not to believe in God, they do not thereafter believe in nothing. They then become capable of believing in anything."—G.K. Chesterton

This isn't just philosophical drift—it's managed decay: truth traded for identity, biology for feeling, meaning for narrative, until reality itself starts to split. We saw it in 2020 when a major network ran the line "Fiery but mostly peaceful protests" while buildings burned behind the reporter. When words soothe the audience instead of naming the scene, the conscience goes numb.

When truth is replaced, reality fractures further. Universities banned speakers for "psychological safety." Newsrooms rewarded silence over integrity. Even biology itself became a battlefield of offense. Lies became virtue—and virtue became violation.

Today, we don't seek truth—we curate it. We choose sources that flatter us. We dismiss facts that challenge us. We silence voices that convict us. We demand safe spaces from reality itself.

And now, the consequences are visible everywhere—justice politicized, morality performed, faith commercialized, children taught confusion and calling it compassion.

But none of this is compassion. It's cowardice wrapped in kindness. Isaiah gave this warning to a nation that replaced obedience with indulgence: the vines still grew, but they bore wild grapes. Judgment wasn't random; it was rational. When truth was inverted, the vineyard decayed, the walls fell, and exile followed.

Truth has become offensive—not because it changed, but because we did. In a society where everyone claims their own version of reality, what is real becomes the enemy. Because what is unchanging divides. It corrects. It judges. And ultimately, it humbles.

And that is exactly what we need. We don't need more tolerance—we need clarity. We don't need more slogans—we need Scripture.

Freedom isn't the absence of a standard; it's alignment with the One who defines it.

And if we don't reclaim what is real—not just in belief, but in courage—we will raise a generation too fragile to face the world and too blind to recognize what's breaking it.

Reflection:

Where have you traded clarity for comfort? Stayed silent on what is real to protect a reputation? Speak what must be said this week—with love and with strength—not for approval, but for righteousness. Let your words cut through the fog and call your life back to what stands when compromise collapses.

III. Feelings vs. Facts

Feelings are not the enemy—but they're not the compass either.
In today's culture, feelings are elevated above facts. Emotion determines reality. Hurt feelings outweigh hard truth. And the highest virtue is not honesty, but comfort.

But comfort is not the same as healing.

God gave us feelings to experience the world, not to define it. Anger doesn't equal injustice. Attraction doesn't equal identity. Sincerity doesn't equal truth.

One of the most dangerous lies of our time is that being offended means you're right.
Reality doesn't submit to hurt feelings; it demands alignment.

When Jesus said, "You will know the truth, and the truth will set you free," He wasn't offering comfort—He was offering clarity. He spoke to believers trapped in self-deception, showing that freedom comes not from validating emotion, but from submitting to what God has declared. Known truth never chains—it liberates. It exposes sin's illusion and restores direction, turning emotional storms into solid ground.

Look at today's moral battles. When someone speaks plainly—about sin, gender, discipline, or the sanctity of life—they're often canceled, labeled hateful, or pressured to apologize. Even believers fall into this trap.

In recent years, writers who questioned the new gender orthodoxy have been smeared rather than answered—proof that silencing doesn't erase reality; it only reveals fear of it.

More than once in recent years, pastors have apologized publicly for stating historic Christian teaching—proof that the standard didn't change, but the pressure did.

"Truth is not fragile. People are."—Voddie Baucham

If we fail to teach people the difference between feelings and facts, they will mistake collapse for compassion and fragility for virtue.

Christianity is not a feeling-based faith. It is rooted in what is. And what is isn't always gentle—but it is always good.

Your emotions are real. They simply are not the throne. Christ is.

Reflection:

Where have your emotions been driving decisions that should be led by what stands? This week, catch one moment when your feelings rise first—and submit it to Scripture before responding. Offer that act as worship—anchoring yourself to the standard that outlasts offense and brings freedom through its steady strength.

IV. The Seduction of Relativism

Relativism promises compassion—but delivers confusion.
It sounds noble: "You have your truth, I have mine." But the

moment truth becomes individual, it ceases to have meaning. If everything is true, then nothing is. If morality is just perspective, then evil is just a difference of opinion.

"There is a way that seems right to a man, but its end is the way to death." (Proverbs 14:12)
Solomon wasn't warning about ignorance—but deception. "Seeming right" is what makes relativism seductive: it feels compassionate, enlightened, and safe, but it leads straight into ruin. The broad road of moral flexibility always looks merciful at the start—until it ends in collapse. Solomon's wisdom calls us back to the narrow road of reverence, where the fear of the Lord anchors discernment, and the end is not destruction but life eternal.

Relativism masquerades as humility—but it's intellectual cowardice, avoiding judgment's discomfort by pretending equality in validity.
But that's not love. That's abandonment.

If you saw someone walking toward a cliff, would you affirm their journey? Or would you warn them—even if they felt offended?
Truth isn't always comfortable. But it's never cruel.

"Tolerance is the virtue of a man without convictions."—attributed to G.K. Chesterton
Chesterton's line wasn't cynicism—it was diagnosis. When conviction dies, tolerance becomes an idol, and society trades strength for sentiment. Without truth as anchor, tolerance turns to apathy, enabling "anything" belief amid godless drift. Hope begins where conviction returns—where love refuses to lie.

Today's world tolerates everything—except conviction. The man who speaks clearly is shamed. The man who warns is silenced. The man who refuses to lie is labeled a threat.
But truth doesn't adjust to make you comfortable. It invites you to grow.

Relativism doesn't just rot morals; it destabilizes society. Once reality becomes negotiable, policy starts chasing feelings. In the last few years, schools and courts have treated basic language as optional—then disciplined ordinary speech that refused to participate. People didn't always change their minds; many simply learned to stay quiet. When emotion outranks fact, institutions don't explode—they drift into "polite" absurdity: slogans replace standards, intimidation replaces persuasion, and trust erodes without a single riot. Relativism isn't compassion. It's chaos with manners—and it never ends in clarity. It ends in collapse.

This is a new Tower of Babel—every person speaking their own version of reality until no one understands another. And yet, hope remains: when what is real is reclaimed, language, morality, and meaning can be rebuilt.

"The truth will set you free." (John 8:32)

Freedom is not found in self-definition. It is found in submission to reality—to the One who defines it.

Reflection:

Has relativism crept into places where conviction should stand immovable? Have you softened your stance because culture insists certainty is arrogance? This week, speak from a grounded place—not to win arguments, but to steady what's been shaken. Let your words cut through confusion and call your life back to the clarity God demands.

V. Truth and the Nature of God

Truth isn't just a principle—it's a Person.

Jesus didn't say, "I teach the concept." He said, "I am the truth." That changes everything. Because what is real is not merely factual—it is relational. To pursue reality is to pursue Christ. To distort what is real is to distort His image. And to reject what He has declared is to reject the only One who can set you free.

"I am the way and the truth and the life." (John 14:6)

When Jesus said, "I am the truth," He wasn't offering a philosophy to debate. He was claiming authority over reality itself. Truth is not something we possess and rearrange; it is Someone we answer to. And that means following Christ is not merely agreeing with statements—it is submitting your life to the One who cannot lie.

What is real is not detached data floating in space. It flows from the nature of God—holy, unchanging, eternal. This is why relativism collapses under the weight of divine reality. You cannot redefine what God has spoken. You can ignore it, deny it, mock it—but you cannot undo it.

God does not evolve with culture. What He has established does not adjust itself to polls, trends, or emotions. It is not here to flatter us—it is here to form us.

In the next chapter, we'll go deeper into that order—how creation itself testifies that truth is not invented; it's discovered.

Truth is not a tool we wield—it's a reality we submit to. And when we do, it doesn't just inform us—it reforms us, transforming mind and character until we mirror His nature.

To speak truth is to represent Christ; to live truth is to reflect Him; to love in truth is to reveal His heart.

Reflection:

What part of God's character have you softened to keep life comfortable? Are you following a Christ shaped by culture or the Christ revealed in Scripture? Submit now—letting His unchanging nature form you through the real presence that confronts, corrects, and makes you whole.

VI. Tolerant Lies, Intolerant Truths

We're told today that tolerance is love—but only if you agree. The culture that shouts inclusion is quick to exclude anyone who speaks uncomfortable truths. Biblical convictions are labeled hate. Moral clarity is branded bigotry. And truth is only allowed if it bends.

Modern tolerance is not about freedom—it's about control. You are free to speak only if your words conform, free to believe only if belief offends no one, free to worship only if your God stays silent on sin. That isn't tolerance; it's tyranny with better branding.

"They hate him who reproves in the gate, and they abhor him who speaks the truth." (Amos 5:10)

Real love tells the truth.

In parts of the West, public biblical conviction has been treated like criminal speech—proof that "tolerance" often means agreement, not freedom.

In a world where lies are praised and truth is punished, silence is complicity. You cannot love a generation and lie to it at the same time.

"Sometimes even to live is an act of courage."—Seneca

This is not the time for fear. It's the time for faithful defiance—the kind that tells the truth, not to condemn, but to call back.

Jesus offended people—not because He hated them, but because He loved them enough to break the illusion. When He confronted the Pharisees in Matthew 15:1–9, He exposed their "traditions of men" that nullified God's Word. His offense was mercy: truth cutting through hypocrisy to restore worship that pleased the Father.

So must we.

Reflection:

Have you let the fear of backlash mute what needed to be said? What reality are you holding back—even with love—because culture refuses to hear it? Speak with steady courage today. Not to provoke, but to anchor your life in what stands when everything else bends.

VII. Living Truth in Hostile Times

Truth has always been dangerous—not because it's violent, but because it exposes.

Jesus wasn't crucified for healing. He was crucified for revealing.

John the Baptist wasn't beheaded for theft. He was beheaded for calling out sin in high places.

Daniel wasn't thrown to the lions for rebellion. He was thrown in for refusing to bow.

"Blessed are those who are persecuted because of righteousness, for theirs is the kingdom of heaven." (Matthew 5:10)

When Jesus spoke this Beatitude, the crowd expected comfort, not confrontation. Yet He promised blessing to those despised for doing right—inheritance through opposition. The fire that burns up the world's applause becomes the forge that proves eternal belonging.

Living truthfully in hostile times isn't about being loud—it's about being immovable: choosing conviction when compromise feels safer, walking into rooms where silence would protect you, and holding to Scripture when culture demands edits.

We are not the first to face this. And we won't be the last.

The early church didn't spread because it was trendy—it spread because it was true. And the truth, lived boldly, became contagious.

In the 1980s and 1990s, Brother Yun—known as "The Heavenly Man"—was imprisoned in China for preaching the Gospel. Beaten, starved, and humiliated, he refused to recant. And the story of his endurance strengthened courage far beyond his cell. Truth can be opposed—but it cannot be erased.

"He who has a why to live can bear almost any how."—Friedrich Nietzsche

Your "why" must be deeper than fear, applause, or comfort. It must be grounded in Christ, shaped by the Word, and strengthened by eternity.

Because if you don't live truth now, don't expect the next generation to fight for it later.

"It is not enough to believe the truth. You must embody it—in speech, in silence, in suffering."

This world does not need more slogans. It needs more saints. And saints aren't shaped by ease. They're forged by fire.

Prayer:

Lord, make me faithful in a hostile age. Keep me from shrinking back when truth is unpopular. Put steel in my spine and love in my tone. Let my work, my speech, and my home align with what I claim to believe. Give me wisdom to know when to speak and courage to speak when I should. Amen.

VIII. A Life Aligned With Truth

The goal is not just to know truth—it's to live it.

We are called to be living epistles, walking reflections of the Word made flesh. This isn't about quoting Scripture more. It's about embodying what Scripture says—with humility, consistency, and courage.

"Be doers of the word, and not hearers only, deceiving yourselves." (James 1:22)

James wrote those words to a pressured church tempted to hide behind belief without action. His warning was direct: truth unacted becomes self-deception. The mirror of faith must become movement—obedience under pressure—until your life says what your mouth claims.

You can't claim truth and live contradiction.

A life rooted in truth is one under divine authority—unbent by trends, unmoved by pressure, unshaped by culture, yet shaping it through steadfast conviction.

This doesn't mean perfection. It means direction.
It means repenting quickly. Speaking gently but boldly. Living so that even your enemies know what you stand for.

History keeps proving the pattern: when a believer stands firm, their witness strengthens others. Dietrich Bonhoeffer faced Nazi pressure with that kind of resolve—preaching when pulpits went quiet, helping form and train pastors within the Confessing Church, and refusing to treat the state as sacred. Later, imprisoned for resisting Hitler, he held fast to Christ to the end—showing how one steadfast life can steady many under tyranny.

"If you are what you should be, you will set the whole world ablaze."—Catherine of Siena

Catherine's words weren't poetic idealism; they were a charge to live clean, courageous, and useful. Holiness isn't passive. A life anchored in truth becomes a signal fire in a dark age.

This world needs more than clever arguments. It needs people who live with conviction—the kind that isn't seasonal, performative, or self-righteous. The kind that stands when mocked and loves when tested.

That's the kind of man I want to be.

A Word to My Son

If you ever read this, I pray you don't just inherit my beliefs—I pray you surpass them. Live truth whether it's praised or despised—in your words to your mother, your kindness to strangers, your work, prayer, rest, repentance, and leadership. Let your life speak where my words fall short.

If you follow the truth, you'll never walk alone.

Because truth is not just a principle.

It's a Person. And He walks with those who stand for Him.

So build your life on Him.

Reflection:

Where is your life out of sync with the truth you claim? Take one step this week to align your habits, speech, or relationships—not theory, but action—grounding you in embodied truth that endures eternally under divine authority and lived companionship with Christ.

Chapter 6

God, Logos, and Order

I. The Origin of Order

B efore there was chaos, there was order. Before there was man, there was mind.

God didn't just create the universe—He structured it. With laws, patterns, boundaries, and purpose. The ancients called this Logos—reason, meaning, and order at the center of all things.

"In the beginning was the Word, and the Word was with God, and the Word was God." (John 1:1)

"That word, translated 'Word,' is Logos." At its simplest, it means "word" or "message," but John uses it with weight: not mere sound, but the divine Word who is personal, eternal, and active in creation.

God didn't speak chaos into existence. He spoke light, boundaries, and rhythm. "And God said, 'Let there be light,' and there was light. God saw that the light was good, and He separated the light from the darkness." (Genesis 1:3–5)

In that first command, the formless void met divine precision. Light became boundary, and time found rhythm. Creation itself became a sermon: order is not the enemy of freedom—it's the foundation of peace.

"God is not a God of disorder, but of peace." (1 Corinthians 14:33)

Without order, there is no peace. No clarity. No life.

Jesus demonstrated this authority when He calmed a violent storm with a single command: "Peace, be still." The winds obeyed. The sea settled. Nature recognized its Maker.

That same Word still speaks. And where His Word is honored, chaos loses its grip.

This is why the modern world feels so off. When you reject the Creator, you unravel the standard. When you abandon the Logos, you descend into noise—contradiction, confusion, and emotion crowned as truth.

Even engineering shows how small misalignments compound. In 1999, NASA lost the Mars Climate Orbiter after teams failed to convert between imperial and metric units—a preventable mismatch that wrecked the mission. Moral order works the same way: small departures from design don't stay small for long.

Aristotle said everything has a *telos*—a purpose. A chair is for sitting. A knife is for cutting. Man is for reason. But reason is only sound when it aligns with the Source.

The Stoics built their lives around Logos, seeking an order they could sense but not fully name. Epictetus described the aim of life as "to follow God." You know the name. You know where order begins: not in you, but in God.

Christian-Stoic Principle #5—Live According to Nature; Walk in the Spirit

The phrase "live according to nature" was a Stoic way of saying: align your life with reality—reason, restraint, and the moral order they believed was stitched into existence. They called that order Logos. Cicero wrote, "True law is right reason in agreement with nature." He was reaching for a law that transcends culture—a moral architecture stable enough to judge the age instead of being shaped by it.

Christianity clarifies what they sensed and names its Source. Nature is not your impulses. It is God's creation—good in design, fractured by sin, and restored through Christ. So "living according to nature," in the truest sense, is living according to God's intended order: to walk by the Spirit, not the flesh (Galatians 5:16). What the philosophers pursued through discipline alone, God grants through indwelling—order written not only in the world, but in the heart.

Reflection:

Do you see order as optional—or essential? Where have you allowed chaos to rule when God has already provided a blueprint? Align one area this week, and let God's order steady what has been drifting.

II. God Over Chaos

Chaos isn't new. It's just louder now.

From the beginning, Scripture shows God hovering over the deep—a shapeless void. And with a word, He brings form, purpose, and light. That's not just a creation story. That's a pattern. Every time God enters, chaos loses ground.

"The earth was formless and empty... and God said, 'Let there be light.'" (Genesis 1:2–3)

God speaks, and chaos organizes.

But in our world today, people invite chaos and silence the Word. We exalt confusion, reward disorder, and teach that truth is personal and identity self-created—rebellion disguised as progress.

"They exchanged the truth about God for a lie, and worshiped created things rather than the Creator." (Romans 1:25)

Paul wrote those words to a culture that looked sophisticated but was collapsing. Their idols promised liberation but produced futility—darkened thinking, fractured homes, and decaying virtue.

Order is not oppression. It's protection.

When God sets boundaries, He isn't limiting you—He's anchoring you. Just as banks give a river strength and direction, divine structure gives your life stability and clarity. Without it, the waters flood. Chaos reigns.

Even in nature, disorder is unsustainable. And in history, ignored order produces real consequences. In 2020, the Beirut port explosion—driven by dangerously stored ammonium nitrate—killed more than two hundred people and devastated the city. What happens in matter mirrors what happens in morals: abandon structure, and destruction follows.

And yet, the culture calls chaos "freedom."

True freedom is not doing whatever you want. It's becoming what you were created to be.

God is not panicked by the chaos around us. But He will not compete with it. He speaks order—and it's up to us to receive it.

Reflection:

Where have you mistaken chaos for freedom? What boundaries must you restore to live in God's designed order? Reclaim one this week, grounding yourself in divine structure that anchors you with unchanging peace and purpose.

III. Designed to Reason

You were made to think clearly.

That might sound obvious, but in today's world, reason is under attack. Emotion rules, outrage sells, and logic—once a virtue—is now branded as oppression.

But God designed your mind not to react, but to reflect. Not just to feel, but to process, discern, and align.

"Come now, let us reason together," says the Lord. (Isaiah 1:18)

That invitation came to a rebellious nation dripping with ritual yet void of repentance. Their sins were scarlet, their sacrifices empty. God didn't shout over them—He reasoned with them, appealing to intellect and conscience alike: 'Though your sins are like scarlet, they shall be white as snow.' Divine reasoning called them not to emotion but to examination—a logical grace that cleanses and restores clarity where rebellion had clouded thought.

There's a moment in the Gospels where Jesus is challenged by the Pharisees. Instead of launching into argument, He responds with a single question: "John's baptism—was it from heaven, or from men?" They couldn't answer—because they weren't seeking truth. They were seeking control. And truth exposed them.

"The further a society drifts from truth, the more it will hate those who speak it."—attributed to George Orwell
We see this drift even when well known institutions prize rhetoric over standards: when integrity slips, trust collapses. Yet exposure still matters—proof that scrutiny isn't cruelty, and that light can still reach what pride tries to hide.

The Stoics believed in *Logos*—the rational principle that orders the universe. To them, reason was sacred. Discipline of thought was central. But their reason had no Redeemer. You do. The ultimate *Logos* is not abstract principle but a Person—Christ, through whom all things hold together.

Jesus didn't just live righteously. He spoke with clarity, asked piercing questions, and silenced confusion. He is truth—and truth holds up under examination.

"Test everything. Hold fast to what is good." (1 Thessalonians 5:21)
God welcomes scrutiny because truth never fears it.

As Marcus Aurelius observed, the soul slowly takes on the color of its thoughts.

But culture tells you to "live your truth." That's not freedom. That's fragmentation. If everyone defines reality by emotion, there is no shared ground—only noise.

You were not built to live by vibes. You were built to seek truth.
Right thinking leads to right living. Your mind must be renewed to withstand the flood of noise—disciplined, discerning, and devoted to the Word that anchors reason in revelation.

"Do not conform to the pattern of this world, but be transformed by the renewing of your mind." (Romans 12:2)

Your mind is either being shaped by Logos—or hijacked by emotion. One leads to clarity. The other leads to collapse.

Meditation:

Reason Under Discipline
Your mind is powerful—so it must be governed.
Notice the urge to spiral, to prove, to panic, to win.
Return to what is in your control: judgment, intention, action.
Let reason serve virtue, not ego.
Let temperance keep the reins.

IV. The Structure of the Soul

The soul isn't abstract. It's structured.
Modern culture treats the soul like a feeling—emotional, unanchored, undefined. But Scripture shows something very different. The soul has depth, but also design. It's not chaos. It's craftsmanship.

"Love the Lord your God with all your heart and with all your soul and with all your mind." (Matthew 22:37)

Your soul includes your will, emotions, intellect, and conscience. When these are aligned with God, there is peace. When they are divided, there is inner war.

Picture your soul as a house. Your thoughts are the foundation. Your emotions are the windows—they reflect what's happening inside. Your will is the frame. And God's Spirit? That's what fills it with life.

"Guard your heart above all else, for it determines the course of your life." (Proverbs 4:23)

Disorder in the soul doesn't happen overnight. It happens when one part takes over—when emotion hijacks reason, will overrides wisdom, and conscience grows numb. You can see it today in leaders who rise fast but collapse from within—the celebrity who trades discipline for indulgence, the politician who loses integrity to impulse. The soul, once fractured, always exposes itself publicly.

David's story illustrates this vividly. A man after God's own heart—but when he stopped guarding his soul, temptation won. Lust overtook reason. Power overran conscience. His decisions unraveled the structure. When Nathan confronted him, the king didn't argue—he broke. Psalm 51 wasn't performance; it was architecture being rebuilt. God didn't discard him but restructured him—truth in the inward parts, humility replacing pride. His ruin became the blueprint for restoration.

"Create in me a clean heart, O God, and renew a right spirit within me." (Psalm 51:10)

Psychology calls this integration. The Bible calls it sanctification. The Stoics sought harmony in the soul through logic and detachment. They were partly right—disorder breeds despair. But only Christ can reorder what's been broken—not by detachment, but by indwelling.

Your soul wasn't meant to operate in fragments. You were designed to function as one—fully aligned, wholly led.

"An undivided man is a formidable man—not because he's loud, but because he's whole."

You weren't made to live divided. You were made to be whole—and holy.

Reflection:

Is your soul structured or splintered? Which part has taken the lead—emotion, will, intellect, or the Spirit? Rebuild one 'room' this week through prayer, repentance, or discipline—and let wholeness replace the inner tug-of-war.

V. When the World Rejects the Word

When a society unplugs from truth, collapse is only a matter of time.

God's Word is not just sacred—it's structural. It's the framework for justice, identity, family, and freedom. To reject the Word is to reject the blueprint. And what follows is confusion disguised as compassion.

"The grass withers, the flower fades, but the word of our God will stand forever." (Isaiah 40:8)

Isaiah spoke those words to a weary people staring down imperial power and cultural decay. Everything impressive about man was withering; everything rooted in God remained. The point wasn't poetry but permanence: when the winds strip the field bare, the Word still stands—and the people who stand on it do, too.

When the world rejects the Word, it doesn't stop believing. It just starts believing lies.

"They will turn their ears away from the truth and turn aside to myths." (2 Timothy 4:4)

We see it everywhere: feelings over facts, identity without essence, rights without responsibility. Even churches are bending—redefining sin, softening Scripture, preaching affirmation instead of transformation. The recent wave of denominational schisms over biblical authority shows the cost of editing the text to fit the times—division, confusion, and drift.

But truth doesn't evolve to fit the age. It confronts the age and calls it home.

Aquinas said, "Truth is the conformity of the mind to reality." Resisting truth doesn't change reality—it only blinds you to it.

"Your word is a lamp to my feet and a light to my path." (Psalm 119:105)

God's Word isn't just informative. It is directive—revealing and leading, correcting and keeping.

When the Word is rejected, people don't become free; they become lost. When it is received, people don't become smaller; they become whole.

Prayer:

Father, keep me from editing Your Word to fit the times. Correct my thinking where it is modern but not true. Give me reverence before I demand explanations. Help me obey when I understand and when I do not. Plant Your truth in me until it bears fruit under pressure. Amen.

VI. Mystery and Mind: When Logic Isn't Enough

God gave you reason—and He gave you reverence.
Logic matters. Truth matters. But reduce God to a formula and you lose Him; the mind can lead you to the edge, and faith must carry you home.
   "The secret things belong to the Lord our God, but the things revealed belong to us..."—Deuteronomy 29:29
Moses spoke those words at Moab, calling a wavering people back to covenant clarity. "The secret things" honor God's infinite counsel; "the things revealed" bind us to obey what we already know. It isn't anti-intellectual; it's ordered: revelation for obedience, mystery for worship—a path that keeps the mind humble and the heart whole.
   Faith isn't the absence of logic; it begins where logic reaches its limit and trust steps in.
   Think about Job. A man who suffered deeply, asked hard questions, and got no tidy answers—only a whirlwind of divine greatness. That was enough.
Or Thomas. The doubter. Jesus didn't shame him—He showed him.
"Blessed are those who have not seen and yet have believed." (John 20:29)

Reason matters—but reason rightly used knows its limits and bows.

The Stoics sought control through understanding. You are called to surrender through awe.

"I believe in Christianity as I believe the sun has risen—not only because I see it, but because by it I see everything else." —C.S. Lewis

Even mathematics admits its ceiling: in 1931, Kurt Gödel proved that any sufficiently powerful formal system is incomplete—there are true statements it cannot prove. Reason is real, but it isn't final.

God's order is visible—but His nature is infinite. He reveals what you need, not always what you want.

"Now we see in a mirror dimly, but then face to face." (1 Corinthians 13:12)

Let your reason lead you to worship—not pride.

There are things science will never measure: the weight of grace, the power of forgiveness, the presence of the Holy Spirit. Not less real—more.

And the man who walks in faith, not just logic, learns to see with eyes the world cannot understand.

Reflection:

Do you demand understanding before you obey? What part of your journey needs reverence more than reasons right now? Choose one step of obedience this week where you've delayed for certainty—let trust move before clarity, and worship lead your reason.

VII. Rebuilding on the Rock

Order is not something you find. It's something you build.
Jesus didn't just preach truth—He told us where to build. Two men, two houses, two outcomes. One on sand, one on rock. Same storm. Different results.

"Everyone who hears these words of mine and puts them into practice is like a wise man who built his house on the rock." (Matthew 7:24)

Jesus ends the Sermon on the Mount with a builder's warning: both men hear His words; only one obeys. The difference isn't exposure but execution. Same rain, same rivers, same wind—and yet one house stands. Storms don't create foundations; they reveal them.

The storm is coming. Culture will shake. Feelings will fail. Trends will pass. The question is simple: what are you standing on?

The world builds on sand—self-expression, feelings, popularity, politics, and ear-pleasing theology that edits truth. But the Rock is Christ. The *Logos*. The eternal Word made flesh. The unshakable structure that holds firm when everything else collapses.

"For no one can lay any foundation other than the one already laid, which is Jesus Christ." (1 Corinthians 3:11)

We've seen what happens when foundations fail. In 2021, a beachfront condominium in Surfside, Florida, partially collapsed, killing 98 people; federal investigators have identified critical failures around the pool deck and slab connections that began minutes before the tower fell. Small deviations, delayed repairs, unseen weaknesses—when the ground shifts, everything above follows.

This chapter wasn't about abstract theory. It was about the blueprint. If you want a life that withstands chaos, it must be built on divine structure. That includes your time, your habits, your relationships, your work, your screens—the unseen systems that quietly decide who you become.

God is not interested in shallow belief. He wants foundation-deep alignment. Philosophers speak of first principles—foundational truths that shape all others. Jesus is the First Principle. And unlike the shifting ground of this age, He never moves.

"Jesus Christ is the same yesterday and today and forever." (Hebrews 13:8)

To rebuild is not weakness. It's wisdom. If what you built couldn't hold, don't double down on sand. Return to the Rock. Begin where order actually lives:

Structure your days around His Word, not your feed.

Order your commitments around your calling, not your cravings.

Align your boundaries with His convictions, not cultural pressure.

Replace distraction with discipline. Replace emotion as master with truth as master. Replace self as center with Christ as center.

The man who rebuilds on the Rock doesn't just survive the storm—he becomes living proof that God's order still holds. His schedule shows it. His habits show it. His peace under pressure shows it.

Reflection:

What part of your life is still built on sand? If someone studied your daily structure, would they see truth at the center—or convenience? Pick one load-bearing beam this week (time, habit, relationship, or belief) and rebuild it on Scripture—in practice, not talk.

Chapter 7

Virtue, Stoicism and the Christian Life

I. Two Roads to Virtue

C ivilizations across history have pursued virtue—but they have not agreed on where it comes from. In Chapter 2 we defined virtue as moral excellence under God's truth, forged in sacrifice and lived when no one is watching. Here we step into the tension behind that pursuit: some believe virtue is a product of willpower and reason alone; Christianity insists true virtue is the fruit of a new heart. Two roads aim at strength; only one transforms.

"Waste no more time arguing what a good man should be. Be one."—Marcus Aurelius

That's the Stoic call—clean, crisp, admirable. It speaks to the nobility of effort, the power of will, the dignity of integrity. But as C.S. Lewis noted, effort alone cannot produce righteousness; it can imitate it. Without the Spirit, the heart remains unchanged.

Psychologists like Jordan B. Peterson argue that responsibility and disciplined habit create scaffolding for moral growth—helpful but limited. Structure stabilizes; patterns preserve; yet Scripture names a deeper problem: a heart of stone. That needs surgery—the Spirit.

The Stoic Method: Reason, Restraint, and Nature

The Stoics believed that by aligning yourself with *Logos*—the rational order of the universe—you could achieve peace, wisdom, and self-command. They urged men to master emotion, accept suffering, and live with courage in the face of fate.

"He who is brave is free."—Seneca. "No man is free who is not master of himself."—Epictetus

They weren't wrong, just incomplete—Stoicism teaches endurance and points to order; Christ makes new and reveals the Author.

The Christian Call: Surrender, Sanctification, and Spirit

Christianity agrees that virtue matters—but it flips the source. Not will □ virtue, but grace □ new heart □ holy will. It's not suppression of self; it's death to self—not discipline alone, but devotion.

"I have been crucified with Christ and I no longer live, but Christ lives in me..." (Galatians 2:20)

Paul didn't write that as theory but as a man remade. The persecutor fell on the Damascus road, rose baptized, and preached the Christ he opposed. Death-to-self produced a holy will; Stoic endurance yields to something higher—divine indwelling that turns steel discipline into living love.

This doesn't make Stoic virtue useless—it makes it preparatory: a scaffold for minds not yet ready to kneel, a training ground for hearts still trying to earn peace through effort. Reason must bow eventually—not because it fails, but because it finds Someone greater.

The Convergence Point: *Logos* With Flesh

"And the Word became flesh and dwelt among us..." (John 1:14). John didn't present the Logos as a distant principle or philosophical construct. He revealed that the very order the Stoics sensed—the rational structure behind reality—took on flesh. Christ didn't just teach virtue; He embodied it. He didn't point toward a path; He was the path. In Him, the pursuit of order becomes encounter, and the craving for virtue meets its Source. To follow Christ is not to abandon logic, discipline, or psychological insight—it is to place them under their rightful King, where reason is clarified by revelation, discipline is strengthened by grace, and the moral compass is recalibrated toward a Person, not a theory.

Reflection:

What kind of virtue are you building—Stoic or spiritual? Strength rooted in habit or in the Spirit? Name one area where you've relied on sheer willpower, then place it under surrender this week—through prayer, confession, and obedience—trusting grace to transform you through divine empowerment and true soul alignment.

II. The Discipline of the Inner Life

Virtue begins in the unseen.
Before it shows up in behavior, it is shaped in thought. Before it becomes visible to others, it is forged in solitude. And before it becomes consistent, it must be trained.

Discipline is the backbone of the inner life. But it's not just external routines—it's internal mastery. It's the invisible architecture of a mind governed by truth, a heart ruled by peace, and a soul aligned with something higher than impulse.

"He who conquers himself is the mightiest warrior."—attributed to Confucius
That conquest doesn't happen by accident. It requires structure—the kind most men were never taught to build. Executive function—planning, regulating emotion, resisting impulse—is fading in a distracted age. Willpower weakens and habits go reactive without deliberate training, and men excuse the drift as "just my personality."

But order begins inside.
If you do not govern your inner life, something else will.
Daily Structure Builds Spiritual Strength
The Stoics knew this. Marcus Aurelius wrote every morning and every night—not for applause, but for alignment. He ex-

amined his thoughts, rebuked his ego, and reminded himself of what mattered.

"Just that you do the right thing. The rest doesn't matter."

For them, discipline was a moral practice—a way to remain unmoved by chaos. But in Christ, discipline becomes something greater: an act of worship—a declaration of who your Master is.

"I discipline my body and keep it under control, lest after preaching to others I myself should be disqualified." (1 Corinthians 9:27)

Paul wrote into a Corinth obsessed with the Isthmian games. Athletes trained for a perishable crown; he trained for an imperishable one. "Disqualified" wasn't about losing applause but losing credibility—so he mastered the body to guard the gospel, choosing disciplined obedience that forged a testimony stronger than the culture's drift.

Paul wasn't just managing temptation. He was preparing for purpose. You don't train just to feel holy. You train because your calling demands it.

Habit Formation and the Hidden Life

James Clear reminds us that "every action you take is a vote for the type of person you want to become." That's true—but Christianity raises the stakes. Every action reflects whom you serve.

Discipline is not neutral. It either sharpens your alignment with God, or drifts you toward disorder.

Your morning shapes your mind.

Your words shape your witness.

Your private life shapes your public legacy.

"When you pray... go into your room, close the door and pray to your Father, who is unseen." (Matthew 6:6)

In other words—true power is cultivated in silence, not on stages.

The disciplined soul doesn't wait for motivation. It acts with intention, even when the fire is low.

The Fruit of Disciplined Obedience

The modern man scrolls more than he reflects. He plans for the gym more than the soul. He builds bodies while letting the mind rot.

As Cal Newport argues in *Digital Minimalism* (2019), intentional tech habits—a 30-day "digital declutter," value-based tool selection—reclaim attention and purpose, a modern echo of stoic examination and deliberate training.

But the man who trains his inner life:

Thinks before speaking

Resists before reacting

Prays before posting

And repents before rationalizing

He doesn't need external control—because internal order is already present. And that order is not robotic. It's reverent.

A Word to My Son

Discipline will not make you holy—but it will make you available.

It won't save you—but it will keep you steady.

The world will try to sell you shortcuts: dopamine, distraction, half-baked advice about "being yourself." Don't buy it.

The quiet, uncelebrated rhythms of a righteous man will outlast a thousand empty performances.

So build your inner life like a temple—not a tent.

Let prayer anchor your mornings.

Let Scripture shape your worldview.

Let stillness become your sanctuary.

And remember: routine without reverence becomes religion. But discipline fueled by love for God? That becomes character.

Challenge:

Choose one zone—morning, evening, or digital—and restructure it for your inner life. Replace mindless drift with a meaningful rhythm—prayer, a verse, silence—letting discipline become devotion that forges eternal character, steady peace, and a lived testimony.

III. Strength Through Suffering

Suffering is not optional. It is part of being human.
Every life encounters pain—through loss, rejection, failure, betrayal, or illness. The only question is: what will suffering produce in you?
Weak men avoid it. Stoics endure it. Christians redeem it.

"Suffering ceases to be suffering at the moment it finds a meaning."—Viktor Frankl

The Stoics taught that pain was inevitable and that the rational response was acceptance. By mastering your reaction—not flinching, not complaining, not collapsing—you found freedom.

"Difficulties strengthen the mind, as labor does the body."—Seneca

They weren't wrong. But Christianity goes further.
It doesn't just accept suffering—it gives it purpose.
It doesn't only call you to endure—it calls you to become.

The Crucible of Character

Modern psychology confirms what ancient faith has long known: minds are strengthened by adversity. Neuroplasticity—the brain's capacity to rewire—is often triggered by challenge, not comfort.
The same is true for the soul.
Suffering, when submitted to God, becomes a crucible—a furnace where what is false burns away and what is eternal is revealed.

"We rejoice in our sufferings, knowing that suffering produces endurance, and endurance produces character, and character produces hope." (Romans 5:3-4)
Paul wrote to believers pressured by an empire and misunderstood by their neighbors. His chain is deliberate: affliction trains endurance; endurance forges *dokimē*—proven character; proven character births unshakable hope. This isn't optimism—it's evidence of glory ahead, a forward assurance that

outlives cultural despair.

Hope born from suffering is not a mental trick. It's spiritual fire when God stands at the center.

Christ: The Suffering Servant

The Stoics honored strength. But no Stoic imagined that the highest virtue would be found in crucifixion.

Jesus didn't just suffer—He chose it.

He walked straight into it, knowing what lay ahead. He prayed, "Let this cup pass from me... yet not my will, but Yours be done" (Luke 22:42). That is not Stoic detachment—that is divine surrender.

His suffering wasn't senseless; it was salvific.

For the Christian, pain is no longer something merely to survive. Placed in God's hands, it becomes a forge.

Pain with Christ purifies.

Pain without Christ petrifies.

A Word to the Wounded

You are not weak because you feel pain. You are not broken because you cry. You are not failing because you struggle. You are in training.

Even Jesus wept, groaned, and bled.

But He didn't stay in Gethsemane. He went to the Cross.

Because that's where suffering ends—not in despair, but in resurrection.

"No discipline seems pleasant at the time, but painful. Later on, however, it produces a harvest of righteousness..." (Hebrews 12:11)

The Psychological Trap of Avoidance

Pain avoided becomes fear. Pain embraced becomes strength.

The man who dodges hardship grows soft—his mind routes around discomfort and his soul turns reactive, defensive, fragile.

But the man who walks through fire with his eyes on the truth—even when his knees shake—becomes immovable.

Sometimes you don't feel stronger. But the strength is there—revealed not in feeling, but in what you refuse to quit.

Viktor Frankl's logotherapy, forged in WWII camps, showed this plainly: meaning turns pain into endurance. In Auschwitz, he found purpose in serving others and envisioned a future work—proof that embraced adversity can yield resilient strength.

Prayer:

Lord, redeem my suffering. Do not let pain make me bitter or soft. Refine me instead. Give me endurance with humility and strength with obedience. Teach me to carry my cross without complaining and to trust You when the road is heavy. Amen.

IV. The Virtuous Man in Public

Virtue is most tested not in private but in public. It's easy to act righteously in solitude. The real measure is how you hold yourself when the eyes are on you—when pressure mounts, when you're misunderstood, when you're mocked for holding the line. Today we confuse visibility with virtue—applause with good. But the truly virtuous man isn't swayed by applause or pressure. He's anchored in principle, not performance.

Christian-Stoic Principle #3—Four Pillars of Strength; Walk Worthy of the Calling

The classical world taught that a strong life rests on four pillars: wisdom, justice, courage, and self-control. In the Stoic tradition, these weren't moods or motivational traits—they were the architecture of character: a trained way of seeing, judging, and choosing. Wisdom is right judgment. Justice is giving others their due. Courage is endurance under threat. Self-control is rule over appetite and impulse. And they rise together: courage without wisdom becomes recklessness, self-control without justice becomes coldness, and justice without courage becomes cowardice.

Scripture lifts the same pillars and gives them a holy center. It doesn't frame them as self-perfection; it frames them as calling. "Walk in a manner worthy of the calling to which you have been called" (Ephesians 4:1). Not worthy of your image. Worthy of Christ. That means your strength must be clean. Your courage must be righteous. Your self-control must be ordered toward love, not pride. Your justice must be rooted in God's law, not tribal outrage.

One lesson remains timeless: virtue doesn't need a spotlight—and the spotlight often corrodes it. Christ taught the same—give in secret, pray in secret, fast in secret. "Beware of practicing your righteousness before other people in order to be seen by them..." (Matthew 6:1). The inner man matters more than the crowd's opinion. Virtue that depends on being noticed is not virtue; it is performance.

True virtue is not reactive. It doesn't swell with praise or shrink under criticism. It lives upstream of action—the invisible spine that governs speech, decision, restraint. It looks like a father who chooses patience, a leader who owns fault, a worker who stays honest when unseen and when watched, a friend who tells the truth with love, and a man who refuses to trade his conscience for comfort. Strength isn't the absence of power—it's power under control. As Jordan B. Peterson notes, "You're not morally obligated to be harmless—you're morally obligated to be strong, and then to control it." Virtue doesn't mean tame. It means trustworthy.

Today, moral consistency is called intolerance. Strength is labeled toxicity. Biblical virtue is treated as hate speech. We live in a climate where the world applauds contradictions and punishes conviction. This is when pillars matter: not when doing right is easy, but when it costs you.

The Stoics praised poise under pressure—and that's good. But Jesus was never a tame philosopher. He wept publicly. He confronted hypocrisy. He endured torture without revenge. He flipped tables when worship was being profaned. His virtue was not passive; it was courageous love under God's authority. Holiness doesn't blend. It stands apart. If your "virtue" never creates tension, test whether it's real.

And even in public life, conviction still has weight. When enough people refuse to celebrate what they know is wrong, consequences appear—sometimes socially, sometimes economically, always spiritually. The lesson isn't tribal victory. It's that actions carry weight, and standards shape outcomes.

When you walk into a room, bring presence, not performance. Let your peace be felt before you speak. Let your actions confirm your words. And when the world demands your silence, don't raise your voice—raise your standard.

Virtue in public is not a spotlight—it's a compass.

Reflection:

Where have you cared more about virtue's appearance than its reality? Choose one setting (home, work, online) and live for an audience of One—do what's right quietly, document nothing, tell no one—grounding yourself in integrity shaped by divine approval and a holy, unswayed contrast.

V. False Virtue and the Age of Applause

Another trial for the virtuous man is applause. Praise often replaces alignment. Men are rewarded for gestures, not consistency—for signaling, not sacrifice. They say the right things while living the opposite. But false virtue doesn't just deceive others. It deforms the soul.

"The aim of the wise is not to please others, but to live rightly."—attributed to Aristotle

The danger isn't being liked; it's needing to be. When your worth depends on approval, your compass spins to the crowd. You choose what's safe over what's right, and slowly disappear. Virtue that performs isn't virtue. It's theater.

Real virtue doesn't need a platform. It's steady, quiet, inconvenient. It refuses to conform, react, or impress. Jesus wasn't crucified for fitting in. He was crucified for being uncompromising. The same crowd that praised Him demanded His death a week later. Let that warn you: if the crowd defines you, the crowd will destroy you. But if Christ defines you, the world cannot shake you.

So stop chasing image. Stop performing goodness. Start walking in it. Your virtue isn't validated by likes. It's proven in silence.

"Woe to you... you are like whitewashed tombs, which look beautiful on the outside but on the inside are full of the bones of the dead."—Jesus (Matthew 23:27)

Jesus spoke this in the Temple courts His final week, confronting leaders whose polished piety masked neglect of "justice, mercy, and faithfulness." He wasn't condemning public faith but exposing performance—calling them back to obedience for the Father's eyes, not the crowd's. And there's hope in that call: virtue formed in secret endures divine judgment long after public rewards fade.

We are not far from them. Modern virtue often thrives in shallow soil. It doesn't survive pressure. It shifts, not because it's wise, but because it's empty.

"Never call yourself a philosopher... but act in conformity with your principles." —Epictetus

For the Stoic, truth is proved by life, not applause. The man who needs the crowd wears a mask; the man of virtue remains the same onstage and off—showing how embodied integrity exposes imitation when a culture applauds almost anything.

But Christianity cuts deeper: it doesn't just ask if your actions align—it asks if your heart does. "People look at the outward appearance, but the Lord looks at the heart." (1 Samuel 16:7)

You can be kind in public and cruel at home. You can quote Scripture and resent God. You can serve the church and starve your conscience. That's not virtue. That's theater.

This is how we get churches that preach love but avoid repentance, leaders who defend sin in the name of inclusion, and people who silence convictions to protect platforms. Modern virtue makes people feel good, but it doesn't make them holy.

"Am I now seeking the approval of man, or of God?" (Galatians 1:10)

Real virtue costs something. It doesn't just say the right thing—it does the hard thing: standing in the boardroom, speaking truth at the table, holding the line when friends fade. Because righteousness is not a trend. It's a test.

We've seen the pattern: companies win praise for values they never live. Enron's "innovation" mask hid fraud; when truth surfaced, trust collapsed—proof that only heart-aligned consistency rebuilds credibility before people and before God.

Don't mistake applause for alignment. The world will praise you when you echo its values—and crucify you when you don't. The goal is not to be celebrated. It's to be consistent. It's to be holy.

One day, the stage will be gone. The likes will stop. The crowd will forget. But your soul will still speak.

Reflection:

Where have you acted righteous for likes or praise? Write it down honestly. Then do one right thing in secret—no post, no mention, no credit. Pray: "Lord, burn the performative—build the pure," and let that hidden obedience form a steady integrity that can stand before God, rooted in heart-aligned, holy, unwavering consistency.

VI. The Model: Christ Above the Philosophers

Every culture has its heroes. Every generation crowns its thinkers.

Some point to Socrates—who chose death over compromise. Others praise Marcus Aurelius—the philosopher-king who ruled with stoic poise. Many admire Confucius, Seneca, or Epictetus—men who pursued virtue, balance, and reason. Modern voices lift up Jordan Peterson or Viktor Frankl—men who seek truth and responsibility in an age of moral drift.

For all their brilliance, none rise high enough.

Because while the world respects those who explain virtue... it still needs someone who embodied it perfectly.

That someone is Jesus Christ.

Socrates questioned, Confucius instructed, Epictetus drilled self-mastery, Marcus journaled for order, and moderns urge men to "carry the cross" metaphorically—but Christ carried it literally.

He didn't just describe the good—He embodied it. His words were truth, but His life was proof. When discipline needed definition, it wasn't delivered from a lectern; it was carved into history through fasting, obedience, suffering, and forgiveness that held nothing back.

"Great indeed, we confess, is the mystery of godliness: He was manifested in the flesh..." (1 Timothy 3:16)

Paul wasn't composing philosophy; he was bearing witness. The very pattern of godliness walked among us. What thinkers sketched in fragments, the apostles encountered in full. What the wisest men could only intuit, the Son made visible—righteousness with a pulse, virtue with a face, truth in living form.

All virtue, real virtue—flows from Him.

Modern psychology notes that the most integrated lives align thought, behavior, and value; dissonance weakens, alignment strengthens. The Stoics strove for this integration, yet even they fell short of the perfection they sought.

Christ had no dissonance. Every word matched His deeds. He prayed for His enemies. He honored His mother. He taught with clarity, corrected with mercy, and walked toward the cross when everyone else ran from it. His alignment was flawless because His nature was flawless.

"Be perfect, therefore, as your heavenly Father is perfect." (Matthew 5:48)

That's not a call to performance; it's a call to alignment—to wholeness in Him.

Virtue Bridge: Classical wisdom seeks right reason; Christ gives the *mind of Christ*. Classical justice gives each his due; Christ fulfills it with self-giving love. Classical courage endures fate; Christ empowers sons who fear God, not crowds. Classical temperance restrains desire; the Spirit reorders it from within.

The Stoics teach us to master emotion. Christ teaches us to redeem it.

Philosophers point us inward. Christ points us upward.

Psychology offers clarity. Christ offers transformation.

Every great thinker glimpsed pieces of the truth. But none of them was Truth incarnate.

Christ is the North Star of the human soul. To study virtue apart from Him is to study rivers without seeing the ocean they lead to.

Even the Apostle Paul—disciplined, zealous, learned—counted it all loss next to knowing Christ:

"I consider everything a loss because of the surpassing worth of knowing Christ Jesus my Lord..."—Philippians 3:8

Paul wrote those words in chains. From prison he reckoned up his gains—lineage, law-keeping, Pharisaic zeal—and called them loss beside Christ. This was not anti-reason but higher reason: renunciation for greater possession, the "gain" of knowing Him and the resurrection power that turns cultural reach into eternal sanctification.

In the 1940s, C.S. Lewis's BBC wartime talks—later *Mere Christianity*—gave a shaken culture moral clarity, but he refused to let morality become the destination. He pressed the reader past rules and arguments to the living center: not self-improvement, but surrender; not virtue as a badge, but Christ as Lord. The point was never to build better men by willpower alone, but to point broken men to the One who makes them new.

If you study Stoicism—do it. If you study psychology—do it. Learn from the thinkers. Learn from the builders. Learn from the ones who lived with courage. But remember: they were all just men—fallible, flawed, and reaching.

Only Christ lived it fully. Only Christ overcame sin. Only Christ rose from the grave. He is not just the ideal—He is the King.

"The Stoics gave us discipline. Christ gave us redemption. The first refines. The second resurrects."

The pursuit of virtue without Christ may sharpen you, but it will never sanctify you.

Philosophies can instruct your mind, but only Christ can cleanse your heart.

You will find wisdom in many places—but salvation in only one.

Reflection:

Who do you admire most—thinkers who point, or the One they point toward? Have you honored their wisdom more than the Giver? Christ is not another sage; He is the Source. Let Him shape you, lead you, and be enough—the hope of resurrection life transforming virtue from effort into worship.

Chapter 8

Building a Moral Compass

I. Calibrating the Conscience

T he conscience is not true north. It's the needle—and like any needle, it can be bent, dulled, or magnetized by the wrong forces. A misaligned conscience can feel peaceful while walking straight into destruction.

That's the danger of our age: we treat feelings of peace as confirmation of truth, and guilt as oppression. But Scripture warns that conscience is not infallible—it's moldable.
"To the pure, all things are pure... but to the corrupt... their minds and consciences are corrupted." (Titus 1:15).

History proves the point: people have justified slavery, violence, betrayal, adultery, and deceit—and slept at night. They feel at peace—not because they're right, but because their conscience has been shaped by culture, trauma, and self-interest rather than Christ.

Modern psychology calls this cognitive dissonance reduction—the mind's ability to justify behavior and suppress guilt to maintain comfort. The Bible calls it self-deception.
"The heart is deceitful above all things..." (Jeremiah 17:9)
Jeremiah spoke this into Judah's idolatry: hearts engraving sin and then defending it, altars on every hill and trust shifted from the Lord to man. That deceit did more than mislead—it justified evil and bred a curse of barrenness (Jeremiah 17:5-6). But the

prophet also held out hope: the one who trusts in the Lord is "like a tree planted by water," blessed and fruitful (17:7–8). Conscience finds life not in self-trust, but in calibrated trust in God.

Not All Peace Is Righteous Peace

Your conscience is not your god. It's your guide—and every guide needs calibration.

God gave you a conscience to nudge you toward truth, not to define it. A newborn conscience knows very little. It must be trained, sharpened, and formed through Scripture, wise community, reflection, and correction.

When properly aligned, conscience becomes a powerful internal safeguard against sin. But left untended, it will eventually approve what once disturbed you. It will shift with the moral climate you live in—and that climate is often polluted.

Peace isn't the first test of truth. Direction is.

Stoic bridge: Epictetus trained *prohairesis* (the moral will) to judge appearances; that's wise as far as it goes. But Scripture goes deeper—beyond trained judgment to a cleansed heart. Reason can steady the needle; only Christ re-magnetizes it to true north.

Recalibrating in the Modern Age

Today, conscience is curated by content—children by feeds more than Proverbs, adults by podcasts/reels/trends, and discernment outsourced to influencers and pundits instead of Scripture and godly counsel.

As a rule: what you practice, you become—and an untended conscience slowly approves what it once resisted.

Modern case in point: role and culture can mold what people accept. Re-examinations of the Stanford Prison Experiment and the BBC Prison Study show how leadership, identity, and context shape behavior and justification—a reminder that an untrained conscience can learn to approve what it once condemned. Recalibration matters so normalization doesn't become moral numbness.

That's why recalibration is not about guilt—it's about realignment. You don't need to destroy your conscience. You need to restore it to its God-given settings.

That restoration only happens through repeated exposure to God's Word, the correction of trusted believers, honest self-examination, and obedience even when it cuts against your comfort.

A Word to My Son

My son, don't ever silence your conscience—but don't follow it blindly either.

Test it. Train it. Sharpen it.

Expose it to truth like iron sharpens iron. Read Proverbs more than posts. Study Christ more than culture. And when something feels off, don't just ask, "How do I feel?" Ask, "What does God say?"

Because peace without truth is a trap. And guilt that leads you back to righteousness is grace in disguise.

"The conscience is a gift from God—but it's only trustworthy when shaped by His Word."

Reflection:

Where have you equated peace with moral correctness? Write down one belief or habit that feels "right" but may need realignment, then test it with Scripture—building a conscience trained by truth, sharpened by God, and steady in aligned discernment.

II. Principles Over Preference

Conviction doesn't come from preference. It comes from principle.

Most people don't live by principles. They live by preferences—carefully disguised as values. We say we care about truth... until it costs us something. We say we believe in justice... until it challenges our tribe. We say we love righteousness... until it asks us to deny ourselves.

Preference bends when the pressure rises. Principle doesn't. A moral compass built on preference will always point toward comfort—not conviction.

"Everyone did what was right in his own eyes." (Judges 21:25).

That verse isn't praise. It's diagnosis.

Preference Is a Shaky Foundation

When morality is tied to feelings or convenience, it will never hold up in a storm. But when it's anchored to unchanging principles—love, truth, integrity, sacrifice—you gain a strength that doesn't sway under pressure.

Look at Jesus. He didn't please everyone. He didn't even try. He stood on principle—even when it meant being hated, mocked, and crucified. Why? Because truth is not negotiable.

As C.S. Lewis said, "If you look for truth, you may find comfort in the end; if you look for comfort, you will not get either."

"For he flatters himself in his own eyes that his iniquity cannot be found out and hated." (Psalm 36:2). David's warning stands in the same moral landscape as Judges—a culture drifting without direction, where what feels right becomes the standard. Preference persuades in the moment, but it's a mirage; choices that appear compassionate or practical often carry hidden ends that corrode the soul and damage the community. Principle, by contrast, leads through obedience into life, cutting against the wind of the moment to secure an eternal outcome.

Modern Morality Is Personal, Not Principled

We live in a culture that treats truth like a menu—customized, filtered, and curated to taste. We talk endlessly about "values," but often mean "what feels right to me right now." Branding replaces backbone, and preferences get re-labeled as principles.

As Os Guinness observed, "Never have we had so much talk of values, and so little moral clarity."

We don't reject principles outright—we redefine them until they become preferences.

Principles Are Not Opinions

Principles are objective standards rooted in something higher than emotion or convenience. In Christianity, they flow from the unchanging nature of God. That's why they don't move when the culture does. "Heaven and earth will pass away, but my words will not pass away." (Matthew 24:35). As Jordan Peterson warns, "If you betray yourself—if you say untrue things... you weaken your character. And character is destiny."

Courage Without Volume

Mark wasn't loud. He didn't chase attention or argue to impress. In high school he mostly listened—steady, quiet, unnoticed.

One afternoon, a teacher mocked Christianity during class. The room laughed. Mark didn't. He raised his hand and, without irritation or theatrics, quoted Jesus: "Everyone who is of the truth listens to my voice." Silence followed. A few smirked, but he stayed calm—not out of stubbornness, but conviction.

After class, a student approached him and said, "I've never seen someone stand that calmly for what they believe." Mark didn't sway the room. He simply stood straight when others bowed to pressure. Sometimes the strongest voice is the quiet one—the one that refuses to bend.

Christ and the Principle of Obedience

Jesus didn't live by preference. He lived by principle. He didn't feel like being crucified—He chose it. He wasn't praised for telling the truth—He was hated for it. But His principle was obedience, not popularity.

"I do not seek to please myself but Him who sent me." (John 5:30)

And if you follow Him, you're not just called to believe nice things. You're called to embody eternal things—even when they hurt.

A Word to the Reader

Don't trust your preferences. They will shift with your mood, your relationships, and your circumstances. Principles are harder—but they are holy.

You may lose applause. You may lose comfort. You may even lose relationships. But what you gain—integrity, strength, peace before God—cannot be stolen.

Live by principle, not vibe. Live by truth, not trend. Live by the Word, not by the crowd. Because only one of those will still be standing when the storm comes.

"Preference changes with pressure. Principle only sharpens."

Challenge:

Audit your moral framework this week. Write three values, then ask: Have I lived these when it was costly? Would I still hold them if I had to stand alone? If not, strengthen them—rooting your principles in God's truth so they anchor you with unshakable conviction when preferences shift.

III. The Role of Repetition in Moral Clarity

Repetition forms your reality.

We like to think we're shaped by big moments—breakthroughs, epiphanies, rock-bottom realizations. But in truth, we're shaped more by what we repeat than what we remember.

"Do not let this Book of the Law depart from your mouth; meditate on it day and night..." (Joshua 1:8)

Joshua received this charge on the edge of the Promised Land, leading a people formed by forty years of wandering. "Meditate day and night" was a battle plan, not poetry: daily recitation and remembrance so obedience becomes reflex. Prosperity and success were tied to repeated alignment—truth reinforced until it held steady against every cultural crosswind.

Repetition Trains the Conscience

Every time you choose discipline, speak truth, or resist temptation, you train your moral reflex. Like a fighter drilling combinations until they are second nature, righteousness is built one rep at a time.

Your habits either dull your conscience or sharpen it.

Seneca wrote, "We become brave by doing brave things." Aristotle said, "Excellence...is a habit. We are what we repeatedly do."

Virtue isn't theory. It's practice.

A True Account: John in the Warehouse

John worked overnights—alone, tired, no cameras—easy chances to steal time or tools. He prayed before each shift, quoted one verse as he clocked in, and treated the job like it mattered to God.

After six months the manager said, "You're the most trustworthy guy here—and I don't even know why."

John did—repeated principle that built a reputation no speech could.

Why the World Repeats Lies

The world pushes a single, ceaseless catechism—scroll here, like this, crave that—because repetition shapes belief. In 2021, Facebook whistleblower Frances Haugen testified that engagement-driven algorithms reward outrage and distortion; the fallout intensified public scrutiny and fueled bipartisan pressure to reform how platforms are designed and governed. So if the world trains people to compromise, we must train ourselves to stand.

"Do not conform to the pattern of this world, but be transformed by the renewing of your mind." (Romans 12:2)

Repetition Is Discipleship

You're always being discipled—by Netflix, TikTok, Scripture, or silence. The question is: by what, and toward what?

Tell the truth once, it feels awkward. Tell it a hundred times, it feels natural. Lie a thousand times, and your conscience won't even flinch.

"Do not be deceived: God cannot be mocked. A man reaps what he sows." (Galatians 6:7)

You can't reap virtue if you've been sowing compromise—even in small things.

The Power of Spiritual Rhythm

Scripture repeats commands—not because God forgets, but because we do:

"Remember the LORD your God..." "Write them on your heart..." "Teach them diligently to your children..." "Day and night...meditate on it..."

"I have hidden your word in my heart, that I might not sin against you." (Psalm 119:11). Not posted it. Not debated it. Hidden—memorized, repeated, rehearsed until it became part of him. Your compass isn't set once. It's set daily.

Stay the Course

Don't underestimate the small choices you make every day. They are forming your default settings for the moment you're tested.

One day, when a split-second decision determines your integrity, you won't have time to think—you'll simply act on what you've trained. Make sure your training points to truth.

Meditation:

Repetition Builds Character

Picture a stone shaped by water—steady, not sudden.

Your habits shape you the same way. Choose one virtue to practice today: wisdom, justice, courage, or temperance.

Hold it like a compass point. Let repetition make the good familiar—and the wrong less attractive.

IV. Teaching the Next Generation to Navigate

A compass only matters if you know how to use it.

Today's kids aren't morally lost because they're bad—they're lost because no one taught them to read the map, handing them screens, slogans, and therapy-speak instead of structure.

"Start children off on the way they should go, and even when they are old they will not turn from it." (Proverbs 22:6)

You can't outsource moral formation to culture. You either teach it—or the world will.

Christian–Stoic Principle #6—Expand Your Responsibility; Love Thy Neighbor

A wise life widens its circle of concern—from self to family to community and beyond. True maturity means owning responsibility for more than your comfort. Ancient virtue ethics spoke of duty through roles: son, brother, citizen, worker. As character matures, responsibility expands. Scripture doesn't shrink that vision; it completes it: "You shall love your neighbor as yourself" (Matthew 22:39). Walking in the Spirit means letting responsibility expand—first at home, then outward—not as control, but as care. Your conscience isn't fully formed until it considers how your choices shape the souls around you.

Navigation Requires Direction and Example

A child doesn't just need rules. He needs a reason. He needs to see why righteousness matters and how it's lived when no one is watching.

One father told his teenage son: "Integrity is doing what's right when it's hard, even if it hurts your pride." Weeks later, the boy returned money a friend had stolen—and when asked why, he simply said, "Because of what you said."

Moral clarity doesn't come from lectures. It comes from legacy. Aristotle's Nicomachean Ethics echoes this: we become just by doing just acts, learning virtue through imitation and habituation—apprenticeship before articulation.

Think of Malala Yousafzai. After being shot for seeking an education, she and her father kept modeling courage—and that daily, embodied conviction rippled far beyond one home, forcing the world to look at what it tried to ignore. That is what example does: it multiplies. Courage isn't celebrity. It's consistency—especially at home.

Don't Just Condemn the Fog—Show the Way

We don't need more shouting about what's wrong with Gen Z, but more examples of what's right.

Show them men who live with discipline. Show them women who walk in truth. Show them marriages where forgiveness wins, and parenting where Scripture guides.

Jesus didn't just say, "Follow the rules." He said, "Follow me."

"In everything set them an example by doing what is good." (Titus 2:7)

Paul wrote this into a culture of confusion, calling Titus to teach by doing—soundness of life that young believers could imitate when the winds pushed the other way. This is moral clarity as apprenticeship: not merely explained, but embodied—so integrity becomes transferable across generations by the power of God.

Children Learn Morality From You

Kids and young adults are watching more than they're listening. If you lie to avoid conflict, they'll learn cowardice. If you cheat "just this once," they'll learn entitlement. If you preach righteousness but model compromise, they'll learn hypocrisy.

And eventually, they'll walk away—not from God, but from the version of God you modeled.

A Word to My Son

I will not just protect you—I will prepare you. This world is filled with false lights. You'll be told to follow your heart, your friends, your feed. But you must learn to follow truth.

When you feel lost, don't panic. Look for the map. Open the Word. Seek counsel. Pray hard. And remember what I've lived in front of you—not just what I've said.

Because one day, you'll be the compass for someone else.

Reflection:

What are you modeling for the next generation—in action, not advice? Write one principle you want to pass on, and one behavior you'll change so it's believable—building a legacy of clear direction through divine example, generational integrity, and lived apprenticeship.

V. The North Star Is Not You

You are not your own moral authority.

That's a hard truth in a culture built on slogans like: "Live your truth." "Follow your heart." "You do you." "Only you know what's right for you."

It sounds empowering. But it's a lie. Because if everyone is their own compass... then we're all lost.

Subjective Morality Isn't Morality—It's Chaos

When morality is based on personal feeling or cultural mood, there's no true North. What feels "right" to one man can feel oppressive to another; what's praised in one era is condemned in the next; what's legal today may be evil tomorrow.

Without an objective standard above human emotion, morality becomes power dressed as virtue. Chesterton said it plainly: lines must be drawn. We erased them—and now people call themselves good by comparison, not by truth.

God Is the Anchor, Not an Accessory

Morality isn't created. It's revealed. We don't invent right and wrong—we discover it, align to it, and submit to it.

"The fear of the Lord is the beginning of wisdom." (Proverbs 9:10)

That doesn't mean blind obedience; it means reverence first—the humble admission that we aren't the final judge. You don't have to understand every command to obey it, or feel it to follow it. The standard isn't you. The standard is God—eternal, holy, unchanging.

Why Self-Defined Morality Always Collapses

Psychologists call it motivated reasoning—the habit of bending evidence toward desire. It's how people justify sin as "growth," betrayals as "being true to myself," and a numbed conscience as "evolving." "The heart is deceitful above all things and desperately sick; who can understand it?" (Jeremiah 17:9). Jeremiah warned in a generation blind to its own drift—a culture where self-trust felt noble while destruction grew underneath. Preference persuades in the moment, but it's a mirage: self-authority walks toward ends it cannot see. God's way is not a vibe but a road—anchored, life-giving, and clear to those who fear Him. Hope doesn't rise from feeling more but from bowing sooner; reverent submission forges direction that endures when the culture thrashes.

If your compass always points to what's comfortable—you're not using a compass. You're using a mirror.

You Were Made to Follow Something Greater

The world says look within. Scripture says look up.

You were never designed to be your own North Star. That weight is too heavy; that authority isn't yours. Even the Stoics, for all their inward discipline, aimed the self at a higher order. Only Christ reveals that order—and embodies it. He is not one option among many. He is the way, the truth, and the life (John 14:6). He doesn't ask you to invent morality; He asks you to walk in it.

A Word to My Son

Son, you are not your own North Star. You are the navigator, not the point of reference. The day you think you can guide yourself without Him is the day you begin to drift—and the current is stronger than you think.

Check your compass often. Align it to the One who does not change. And when you're unsure, don't trust the feeling—trust the fixed point.

Because one day you'll guide others. And if your compass is even slightly off, you won't just lose yourself—you'll lose them too.

Prayer:

God, I submit my moral compass to You. Forgive me for making myself the standard. Align my conscience with Scripture, not preference. Give me the courage to obey truth when it costs and the humility to repent quickly when I fail. Lead me in the straight path. Amen.

Chapter 9

Temptation, Suffering, and the Soul

I. The Anatomy of Temptation

Temptation seldom storms the gates. It slips in quietly, looks harmless—sometimes even good—and then bends truth just enough to make room for desire. It softens God's commands, minimizes consequences, and nudges you into isolation where the whisper grows: You can handle this. You deserve this. No one will know.

Eve didn't see death when she looked at the fruit; she saw something "good for food and pleasing to the eye" (Genesis 3:6). That's the oldest trick in the book: "Did God really say…?" (Genesis 3:1). The serpent distorted God's word, reframed a boundary as a burden, and recast desire as wisdom until the forbidden looked necessary (Genesis 3:1–6).

The hope is just as old: recognize the tilt early, refuse the reframe, and let obedience—not justification—break the chain before it hardens.

I've seen it happen to good men. A man gets a friendly message from a coworker—nothing explicit, just conversation. He tells himself it's harmless. Then, one day, he deletes the thread so his wife won't see it. That's the turning point. The moment it's hidden, temptation has already taken root, and the harvest won't be sweet. What begins as "normal" compromise doesn't stay private for long—it teaches a pattern that spreads to homes, communities, and the next generation.

We've watched the same pattern on a larger scale in the #MeToo era: years of quiet justification exposed in public, where secrecy didn't just conceal wrongdoing—it protected systems. Light is painful, but it's the beginning of untangling chains. And on the personal level, early confession is often the cleanest cut—severing the hook before compromise starts to feel natural.

By the time the moment of choice arrives, the heart's rehearsals have preloaded justifications and set the path. Yet even here, God promises a way out (1 Corinthians 10:13). Act early: shut the door before invitation becomes a chain; bring it to light before secrecy becomes a story you can't stop telling yourself.

Reflection:

When temptation last came, how early did you recognize it? What will you do at the first sign next time—seek help, confess quickly, or change your setting—holding to God's provided escape and letting vigilant discipline forge unchained alignment, a clean conscience, and obedient, transformed living?

II. The Slow Poison of Compromise

Compromise is compound interest on small disobediences. You underpay faithfulness by pennies—attention, honesty, prayer—and the debt grows in the dark. By the time the bill arrives, the balance owns you.

"Do not give the devil a foothold." (Ephesians 4:27).
Every compromise is a foothold—a patch of ground where the enemy plants a flag. Paul warns an embattled church that anger left overnight becomes a landing strip for the enemy: irritation hardens into bitterness, words sour, the Spirit is grieved, and

relationships decay (Ephesians 4:26–32). Hope is urgent and practical—deal with it quickly, forgive fast, and reclaim the ground before a foothold calcifies into a habit.

The Stoics understood this in the language of habit: you become what you repeatedly do. Seneca warned, "the mind is slow to unlearn what it has been long taught." His warning is a sober call to vigilant *unlearning*: when compromise has been your teacher, resist its syllabus—replace reflex with discipline so obedience reclaims ground apathy quietly occupied.

Modern Compromise Looks Respectable

Today's culture dresses compromise well—"self-care" as indulgence, "keeping the peace" as cowardice, "open-mindedness" as moral apathy. We baptize avoidance as wisdom, call refusal to confront sin "kindness," and label chronic disengagement "protecting my energy." But withdrawal from what God has called you to is not balance; it's drift. Over time, this quiet retreat dulls the soul like any other concession. The alternative is full-presence obedience: showing up with integrity where God has placed you, before numbness hardens households, workplaces, churches, and communities—echoing Ephesians' call to reclaim ground before apathy becomes a stronghold.

Jesus did not say, "Be nice so everyone likes you." He said, "Take up your cross and follow Me" (Luke 9:23). And the cross does not fit in the pockets of the comfortable.

The Longer You Wait, the Harder It Gets

A slightly bent compass still feels straight at first. Walk long enough, and the curve becomes conviction. That's why repentance isn't a one-time event; it's a daily discipline.
Like a gardener pulling weeds before they root, deal with compromise while it's small. Wait, and the roots will own the soil.

A Word to My Son

Son, never call a foothold "no big deal"—settle small debts quickly with confession, forgiveness, and course-correction before interest turns them into liens on your life. Keep short accounts with God and people. Stay fully present where you stand. And remember: hard obedience today is cheaper than soft compromise tomorrow.

Meditation:

The First Compromise
See the "small door" you keep cracking open. Notice how harmless it feels in the moment.
Now see the pattern it becomes when repeated. Close it with a calm sentence: "Not me."
Courage is often quiet. Temperance is often private. Stay until the decision feels settled.

III. When Suffering Finds You

Suffering rarely asks permission. It arrives uninvited—through loss, betrayal, illness, or the collapse of something you thought was secure. You don't get to schedule it or choose its form. But you do get to choose your response.

The world often treats suffering as something to escape at any cost. Discomfort is labeled failure; pain, injustice. Yet Scripture treats suffering as a forge—a place where endurance is built and character refined. "Count it all joy... when you meet trials of various kinds," James writes, "for you know that the testing of your faith produces steadfastness. And let steadfastness have its full effect, that you may be perfect and complete, lacking in nothing" (James 1:2-4). This was no poetic exaggeration but a progression: trials train endurance; endurance forms maturity; maturity reveals a faith strengthened beyond circumstance—because endurance anchors the soul in God, not in comfort.

Christian–Stoic Principle #7—Preferred, Not Required; Contentment in Christ

The Stoics taught that suffering is intensified when you insist comfort is necessary. They separated what is preferred from what is required. Health, ease and stability are preferred. But none of them are required for virtue. When desires are held loosely—preferred, not required—pain loses some of its power to rule you, and the soul becomes resilient.

Christian faith deepens that clarity and anchors it in a Person. "Godliness with contentment is great gain" (1 Timothy 6:6). You are not commanded to enjoy hardship, but to refuse its lie—the lie that peace depends on circumstance. Paul said he learned contentment in plenty and in want, not because he was numb, but because Christ was sufficient (Philippians 4:11–13). Discipline can produce steadiness. Faith produces something stronger: trust in a God who is still good when life is not.

Viktor Frankl observed that meaning can transform agony into inner freedom. Epictetus taught that while we cannot control what happens, we can control how we meet it. Together they point toward a truth Scripture fulfills: suffering need not make you bitter; contentment can make you unbreakable. The Christian "why" is not self-invented purpose. It is Christ Himself—His presence, His promises, and His resurrection.

I once knew a woman who lost her husband suddenly. The grief was crushing. Friends urged her to distract herself, to keep busy, to move on. Instead, she turned her mornings into prayer and Scripture. She wept honestly and kept showing up when she could barely breathe. Months later she spoke of a strange, deep steadiness—not because the pain had vanished, but because she had met it with trust instead of escape. Over time, her sorrow became compassion, and she became a refuge for others who were breaking.

Jesus promised trouble—and also victory. "In this world you will have tribulation. But take heart; I have overcome the world." (John 16:33). That means suffering is not the end of the story. It is a chapter—sometimes long, sometimes dark—but never purposeless in the Author's hand.

When suffering finds you, the question isn't only, "How do I make this stop?" but, "Who will I become through this?" Answer with faith, and suffering will not be wasted. Hold comfort as preferred, not required—and hold Christ as required, not optional.

Reflection:

Think of a time when suffering came uninvited. How did you respond then—and how will you respond differently now, knowing it is a forge for your soul? Offer up a first step for the next trial—prayer, Scripture, counsel, service—trusting a faith that redeems pain eternally through God's purpose and the endurance He forms.

IV. The Soul That Endures

Endurance isn't merely surviving. It's staying clean under pressure—refusing the shortcuts suffering offers: numb yourself, betray your convictions, blame God, dull your conscience, trade obedience for relief. Trials don't just hurt; they also tempt. And the soul that endures doesn't only withstand pain—it refuses the escape routes that would cost integrity.

"Blessed is the one who perseveres under trial because, having stood the test, that person will receive the crown of life that the Lord has promised to those who love him." (James 1:12)

James wrote to scattered believers under mounting pressure and gave them hope with weight: trials test faith the way fire tests metal. What survives the heat proves what is real. Perseverance doesn't earn the crown; grace sustains perseverance—and perseverance reveals a love for God that holds when comfort disappears. Endurance now. Inheritance then.

The Stoics valued endurance as strength in itself—character proven when fortune turns against you. That's close, but incomplete. Christian endurance goes deeper: it is sustained not by inner steel alone, but by the Spirit of God.

Consider Richard Wurmbrand—a Romanian pastor who spent fourteen years in communist prisons, including years of solitary confinement, for refusing to renounce Christ. Beaten, starved, and tortured, he still prayed for his captors and whispered hymns in the dark. When he was released, he did not hide his scars. He wore them as testimony: a faith no regime could break. His endurance wasn't self-generated. It was Spirit-sustained—quiet defiance rooted in love for God stronger than fear of pain.

Endurance doesn't come naturally. It is built, like muscle, through resistance. Every trial is an opportunity to grow stronger—not only for your sake, but for others who will one day borrow your courage to stand.

If you belong to Christ, your endurance is not powered by sheer will. It is fueled by the Spirit who dwells within you—the same Spirit who sustained the apostles, the martyrs, and every believer who refused to bow.

Prayer:

Lord, I will not run from what You are using to form me. Strengthen my soul to endure without resentment. Keep me faithful in the waiting, clean in the pressure, and hopeful in the trial. Let my endurance become a testimony. Amen.

Chapter 10

Speak Boldly, Live Humbly

I. The Courage to Speak

Truth-telling has never been safe. It cost prophets their lives, philosophers their freedom, and apostles their blood. Yet every generation is sustained by those willing to speak when silence would be easier.

Socrates drank the hemlock rather than betray his pursuit of truth. The Hebrew prophets thundered warnings to kings who could—and did—strike them down. The apostles preached Christ crucified even as Rome sharpened its swords. What they all understood is what many forget: truth is not a hobby or an opinion. It is a duty.

But speaking truth requires more than boldness; it requires conviction rooted in something unshakable. Boldness without conviction is arrogance. Conviction without boldness is silence. Together, they form the voice that carries light into darkness.

Jeremiah knew this well. He tried to stop speaking, but the truth burned in him like a shut-up fire (Jeremiah 20:9). Even the Stoics sensed the duty: if it isn't right, don't do it; if it isn't true, don't say it. Yet the Christian climbs higher—truth is not merely integrity's measure; it is Christ's very character. To abandon truth is not just to fail yourself. It is to betray Him.

And this is why the pressure in our age is so constant. Culture says, "Stay in your lane." Avoid offense. Prize acceptance over honesty. Wherever silence is rewarded, corruption thrives: in workplaces where fraud is quietly understood, in schools where ideology replaces reason, and in churches where comfort outranks obedience.

Even in the public square, exposure has always been costly. Sometimes one disclosure can force a reckoning precisely because entrenched systems depend on secrecy. Whether in governments, institutions, or families, darkness keeps its power as long as it stays unchallenged. Truth presses outward like fire, refusing to be buried.

Consider Elijah, who believed he stood alone against the prophets of Baal—yet he stood anyway. Consider Paul before Festus and Agrippa, reasoning about righteousness and judgment though he was mocked as insane. Both men knew the cost of truth, and both understood that silence would have been easier. Yet silence would also have been betrayal.

And you will face the same decision—usually in smaller rooms. In conversations with friends. In classrooms. In workplaces. The temptation will be to let a lie pass so you aren't marked by it. But silence, when truth is needed, is not kindness. It is cowardice. Speak boldly, not to win arguments, but to honor Christ. And speak humbly, remembering that the truth belongs to Him, not to you.

"Whoever acknowledges Me before others, I will also acknowledge before my Father in heaven" (Matthew 10:32). Jesus said this while commissioning disciples into hostility, warning them not to fear those who kill the body. The promise is sober and reciprocal: confess Christ on earth, and He will confess you in heaven. Courage's reward is not cultural acceptance, but the smile of God.

Reflection:

When silence feels safer than honesty, what truth are you most tempted to withhold? How will you speak it with courage and grace—trusting God for a faithful voice that endures, backed by divine conviction, heaven's witness, and a life that becomes testimony?

II. The Art of Correction

Correction is one of the hardest acts of love. Anyone can flatter, and anyone can criticize, but few can correct with wisdom. Correction without love is cruelty. Love without correction is indulgence. True correction requires both truth and grace.

"Brothers, if anyone is caught in any transgression, you who are spiritual should restore him in a spirit of gentleness. Keep watch on yourself, lest you too be tempted." (Galatians 6:1) Paul's aim is not humiliation but restoration. The manner is gentleness. The posture is humility. Correction is rescue—pulling someone back before drift becomes destiny.

"Preach the word; be ready in season and out of season; correct, rebuke, and encourage—with great patience and careful instruction." (2 Timothy 4:2).
Timothy is taught a balanced toolkit: correction without impatience, rebuke without pride, encouragement without compromise. The goal is not winning arguments; it is saving souls from confusion.

Even the Stoics understood a piece of this. Seneca noted that a true friend dares to tell the truth. But Christianity raises the stakes: truth-telling is not personal preference—it is responsibility before God. Honesty becomes mercy, not a license to wound.

Correction must be handled with care, because it's easy to get it wrong. Jesus warned against pointing out a speck in your brother's eye while ignoring the plank in your own (Matthew 7:3–5). The problem isn't discerning sin—the problem is correcting from pride. In our time, you can see the danger when a real concern turns into a spectacle: screenshots shared, private failures turned into public entertainment, people eager to "expose" instead of restore. What started as accountability becomes a mob, and even legitimate rebuke loses its power because pride takes the stage.

Wise correction rebuilds what sin has damaged. It doesn't burn down reputations for sport. It fights for the person.

A father notices his teenage son slipping into destructive habits online. He could avoid the conversation to "keep the peace," or he could explode in anger. Both fail. Instead, he chooses the harder path: firm but calm, honest about his own past weakness, opening Scripture, and making love his motive. His correction doesn't crush; it guides. It closes doors the enemy would gladly pry open later.

A Word to My Son

Correction will not make you popular. But if you care more about someone's soul than their opinion of you, you will learn how to speak truth in love. Do it privately when you can. Do it humbly always. And remember: the goal is not to be right—it's to help them come back.

Reflection:

When you see someone drifting, what keeps you from stepping in—fear of their reaction, or fear of being exposed? Ask God for wisdom to balance truth and grace, and for the humility to restore rather than win—so your correction becomes rescue, carrying lasting clarity through divine responsibility and practiced mercy.

III. Humility Without Silence

Humility is not silence. Too often, humility is mistaken for re-treat—as if the humble man has nothing to say, no convictions to stand on, and no courage to act. But Christ, the very picture of humility, also spoke with authority that shook kingdoms. True humility is not the absence of voice but the submission of voice to God.

"Speak the truth in love." (Ephesians 4:15)
Paul urged this into a church fraying at the edges, call-ing believers to grow up into Christ the head. Truth-loving speech was the path to maturity: words that build the whole body, aligning heart and doctrine to Him. This is humble bold-ness—speech that serves unity because it bows to Christ first, not to ego or applause.

Humility requires speech. It is possible to be arrogant in si-lence—hoarding truth out of pride or fear of rejection. It is also possible to be humble in boldness—speaking gently because the truth is God's to deliver, not ours to brandish.

The Christian recognizes this, and even the Stoics nodded toward it: Epictetus prized quiet integrity over boasting, yet warned that error spreads when the good keep still—honesty as responsibility, not a license to wound.

But correction and witness must be offered carefully. When the goal shifts from serving the other person to proving your-self right, you're no longer helping—you're just attacking. We've watched how public pile-ons smother conversation: comedi-ans faced boycotts and venue pressure over material some found offensive, and the debate turned from ideas to silencing. Graceful truth preserves discourse; it can name error without dehumanizing, rebuild trust without performing outrage.

A young woman in a university class listens as her professor mocks faith. She could remain quiet to protect her grade, or lash out in anger. Instead, she speaks calmly, offering a rea-soned defense of belief. She does not win applause, but she earns respect. Her humility is not in silence but in tone—refusing to mirror arrogance with arrogance.

Son, never confuse cowardice with humility. You will be told that keeping quiet is noble, that avoiding offense is wisdom. But wisdom is not the same as retreat, and humility is not the same as fear. Speak when called, even softly, even briefly—but speak. And when you do, let your words be free of vanity. Let them carry weight because they are tethered to the truth of Christ, not the approval of men.

Christ Himself, though "gentle and humble in heart" (Matthew 11:29), overturned tables when His Father's house was defiled. Humility bows before God, not before lies.

Prayer:

God, make me humble without making me silent. Remove vanity and fear. Teach me to correct with love and to confront without pride. Let my words be truthful, timely, and restrained. Use me to build, not to bruise. Amen.

Chapter 11

The Righteous Man in the World

I. Strength in Babylon

Righteousness is tested most when the world around you crumbles. It is easy to be faithful when surrounded by saints, but what about when you live in Babylon—a culture that mocks your God, seduces your desires, and pressures you to conform? To be righteous there is not weakness. It is strength.

Daniel stood at the gates of Babylon as a young man taken captive—stripped of home, freedom, and even his name. Yet what Babylon could not take was his allegiance. Before lions, before decrees, before headlines, he faced a quieter test: appetite and agreement. He resolved not to defile himself with the king's food, even though refusal could cost him his life. That "small" act revealed a strength greater than armies: the strength to obey God when compromise would be easier.

Jesus is the ultimate example. He lived among corruption yet remained undefiled. He ate with sinners without joining their sin, confronted hypocrites without becoming cruel, and endured betrayal without becoming bitter. His righteousness was not isolation but presence—holiness lived in the middle of what was broken. To follow Christ is to walk the same path: in the world, not of it.

The Stoics spoke of endurance in hostile conditions. Marcus Aurelius wrote of the "inner citadel"—a fortress no enemy could conquer. Their fortress was reason; the Christian's fortress is God Himself. "The name of the Lord is a strong tower; the righteous man runs into it and is safe" (Proverbs 18:10). To run there is not retreat but refuge—an anchored soul that can stand without rage and refuse without fear.

Today, Babylon wears different clothes: the workplace that pressures you to sign what you don't believe, the classroom that punishes honest conviction, the social circle that rewards silence and mocks restraint. The righteous do not hide, but they also do not posture. They stand—quiet, steady, unbought.

A Word to the Reader

Your Babylon will not look like Daniel's, but it will test you just as surely. Do not wait for easier days. Resolve now, as Daniel did, that no matter the table set before you, your strength will not be borrowed from the world. It will be drawn from God.

Reflection:

What is your "Babylon" now? Where is the greatest pressure to compromise, and how will you stand firm—without arrogance, with quiet strength—trusting the Lord as your tower?

II. The Radiance of Righteousness

Righteousness is not hidden; it shines. Light may be resisted, but it cannot be denied. A righteous life radiates outward—especially in dark places.

Daniel's faith was recognized by kings who did not serve his God. Joseph's integrity was so evident that Pharaoh entrusted him with authority. Jesus taught, "Let your light shine before others, that they may see your good deeds and glorify your Father in heaven" (Matthew 5:16). This is not self-display. It is God-display—obedience so visible that praise rises past the servant to the Father.

The Stoics observed something similar. Seneca described the virtuous life as a steady fire, unshaken by storms. But the Christian knows the flame is not self-generated. Without the Spirit, we flicker; with Him, we endure.

And the radiance is usually not dramatic. It is daily obedience: the worker who refuses to cut corners, the father who keeps his word, the student who chooses honesty over the easy grade. The righteous man doesn't chase attention, but righteousness itself becomes noticeable.

Sometimes it looks almost invisible: returning the extra change when no one would know, refusing to laugh at what is cruel just to belong, telling the truth when a lie would be easier, apologizing first when pride wants to win. These choices don't trend, but they shine—and over time they do what arguments cannot: they rebuild trust in a world trained to expect hypocrisy. People may not call it holy, but they can tell when it's real.

That light will also draw resistance. Darkness hates exposure. Jesus warned that those who belong to Him will be opposed (John 15:18–19). Yet even under pressure, righteousness speaks. Paul and Silas sang hymns in prison, and their steadiness became a witness stronger than their chains.

Righteousness multiplies. One man's integrity often gives others courage. Shadrach, Meshach, and Abednego stood together and strengthened each other, and their faith still speaks generations later. Your obedience may feel solitary, but it is never without consequence.

A Word to My Son

Do not underestimate the ripple of a righteous choice. You may think your obedience is small, but people are watching. Live so that your life itself is a testimony. And when the world demands compromise, let your steady faith answer before your mouth ever needs to.

Prayer:

Lord Jesus, make my life a light. Form habits that honor You when nobody applauds. Let my consistency preach louder than my opinions. Give me courage to do good quietly and strength to resist sin quickly. Keep me clean, steady, and useful. Amen.

Chapter 12

Rebuild the City

I. Trowel and Sword

Christian–Stoic Principle #8—Memento Mori; Number Your Days (Eternal Aim)

Death is not meant to depress you. It's meant to direct you. Memento mori—remember you must die—was never meant to make a man morbid. It was meant to awaken him. When you remember life is finite, you stop treating distraction like it's harmless and start living deliberately, because you finally see what time is: a stewardship.

Scripture calls this wisdom, not sorrow: "Teach us to number our days that we may get a heart of wisdom." (Psalm 90:12). Numbering your days doesn't make you dark. It makes you clear. A short life demands purpose, and purpose demands courage.

Christianity carries the same urgency and adds the full horizon. Death is not the final wall; it is the doorway into judgment or joy. You will stand before God with the life you built—not your intentions, not your opinions, not your distractions—your life.

This is why delay is so deadly. The enemy loves delay because it feels harmless. It whispers "later" until later becomes never. You don't have time to wait for a perfect season to repent, to lead, to pray, to discipline your body, to rebuild your marriage, to raise your children, to stop the sin you already know is killing you. Delay is how callings die quietly.

That's why Nehemiah matters.

Nehemiah returned to a ruined Jerusalem and didn't merely grieve the rubble—he measured the moment. He acted like time mattered. He rebuilt like the days were numbered. And when opposition rose, he refused to choose between building and defending. He did both.

"So we built the wall... and all the wall was joined together." (Nehemiah 4:6)

"...each labored on the work with one hand and held his weapon with the other." (Nehemiah 4:17)

That is what memento mori is supposed to do to a man: put a tool in one hand, a weapon in the other, and a mission in his chest. Not terrify you. Not darken you. Awaken you.

The walls of a city tell the truth about its people. Strong walls mean vigilance, unity, and shared protection. Broken walls mean negligence, division, and defeat. Spiritually, our walls have been breached—not because we lacked information, but because we lacked resolve. Gates were left unguarded, and compromise walked in like it belonged.

Nehemiah refused to rebuild in theory. He rebuilt in practice. Mockers sneered, threats gathered, fatigue set in—and he answered with order. Families repaired the sections nearest their homes. Builders stayed armed. Watchmen stayed alert. A trumpet stayed ready to gather the people when pressure hit (Nehemiah 4:18–20). That is the pattern.

If you want to rebuild, start where God put responsibility—not where it looks impressive. Repair what is in front of you: your home, your habits, your church, your street. Righteousness in one household ripples farther than a thousand speeches.

And hear this: my joy isn't in your reading. It's in your resolve. Pages do not build walls. Decisions do. Don't finish this book as a consumer of truth. Rise as a builder of it.

Because every wall worth building is tested. Your faith will be mocked, your motives questioned, your obedience called "extreme," your backbone called "judgment." Let it. Fire proves what's genuine: dross burns; gold remains. Rebuilding is not optional. The alternative is to live among ruins while pretending it's normal.

So do not despise small beginnings. Every act of faith, each word of truth, every choice for righteousness is a stone in the wall. The city will not rise in a day, but it will rise by the faithful, not the proud.

Do not merely admire Nehemiah—imitate him. Do not only honor Daniel's courage or Paul's endurance—practice it. Above all, fix your eyes on Christ, the Cornerstone. Without Him, every wall eventually crumbles. With Him, no enemy finally prevails.

Final Challenge: Reader or Builder?

Will you walk away a reader or a builder? The difference is not what you know but what you do.

For the next 7 days, live with trowel and sword:
Build one stone: one concrete act of obedience you can point to.
Guard one gate: one boundary that denies the enemy easy access.
And each morning pray (Psalm 90:12) until your days feel numbered again—so your life starts feeling eternal on purpose.

Rise. Rebuild. Trust the Cornerstone to bind your work—and let unity in truth turn ruins into refuge.

Field Manual

The Battle-Ready Canon

N ot slogans—steel. Not *vibes—formation. This manual puts Scripture in your hands as tools, weapons, and a map for rebuilding your mind, your will, and your home.*

Why a Field Manual?

Every war starts in the mind. Before behavior breaks, belief bends. Lies dress up as compassion. Distraction poses as freedom. Algorithms turn preferences into prisons. You don't drift into truth—you train for it. Training needs a plan. This manual keeps that plan simple and doable for anyone, including those new to faith.

How to Use This Manual (Start in 3 Minutes)

Daily Drill (3–10 minutes)
1. Read the assigned passage. If you can, read it aloud.
2. Name one lie it exposes. Write: "The lie is …".
3. Replace it with truth plus one action today: "Because this is true, I will …".
4. Before bed, add one line: Did / didn't; next step is ….

Weekly Drill (12–20 minutes)
· Rehearse your memory verses (see "Memory Core").
· Review your week: inputs, choices, peace/clarity 1–5.
· Reset: cut one distraction; keep one discipline.

Monthly Drill (30–45 minutes)
· List the top lies you fought; pair each with a verse.
· Re-anchor rhythms at home (table, prayer, Scripture).
· Confess what you dodged; choose one new obedience.

Tools You'll See Here

· Truth Reps—one verse repeated, prayed, and applied for 60 seconds.
    · Lie Audit—a quick inventory of mental traps.
    · Gatekeeping—curate your inputs (screens, voices, rooms).
    · Family Mode—make the table a training ground.

The Canon: Four Pillars, One Spine

These aren't random favorites—they build a steady life.
Pillar 1—Romans (Foundation: 1–8; 12)
Read: 3:21–26; 5:1–5; 6:11–14; 8:1–4, 14–18; 12:1–2
Truth: Justified by grace through faith. No condemnation. Adoption. Renewed mind.
Lies Confronted: "I am my failures." "I can't change." "Feelings define truth."
Prayer: Father, thank You for no condemnation in Christ. I present myself to You. Renew my mind.
Truth Reps: Rom 8:1; Rom 12:2.
Act Today: One visible step that matches adoption (confess, apologize, Scripture before screen).
Pillar 2—John & Isaiah (Identity & the Cross)
Read: John 1:1–14; 8:31–36; 14:6; Isaiah 53:3–6
Truth: Jesus is the Word made flesh—the Way, the Truth, and the Life. By His wounds we are healed.
Lies Confronted: "Truth is hate." "God only tolerates me." "Many paths, same God."
Prayer: Jesus, You are truth. Expose deception in me and heal what sin has warped.
Truth Reps: John 8:32; Isaiah 53:5.

Act Today: Trade a 'peacekeeping' silence for one truth-in-love action.

Pillar 3—Matthew 5 (Character)

Read: 5:1–12; 27–30; 33–37; 43–48

Truth: Kingdom character is upside-down strength—purity, integrity, mercy, enemy-love.

Lies Confronted: "If I didn't do it, I'm fine." "It's okay to hate enemies." "Words don't matter."

Prayer: Lord, form the Beatitudes in me. Clean my inner life. Teach me to love enemies.

Truth Reps: Matt 5:8; Matt 5:37.

Act Today: One private act of purity; one public act of integrity.

Pillar 4—Hebrews 10–12 (Perseverance)

Read: 10:23–25, 36–39; 11 (highlights); 12:1–11

Truth: Do not shrink back. Run with endurance. The Father's discipline produces a harvest of righteousness.

Lies Confronted: "Suffering means God is absent." "I can do this alone." "I'm too tired to keep going."

Prayer: Father, strengthen my hands and knees. Train me under pressure.

Truth Reps: Heb 10:23; 12:1–2.

Act Today: Name a weight; lay it down visibly; run lighter today.

Tracks You Can Actually Finish

Pick one. If you miss a day, don't 'catch up'—start where you are. Formation beats perfection.

30-Day Track (10–15 min/day)

· Days 1–16: Romans 1–8 (read Romans 8 twice)
· Days 17–20: Matthew 5 (read twice).
· Days 21–24: John 1; 8; 14; Isaiah 53.
· Days 25–30: Hebrews 10–12 (read twice).

60-Day Track (15–20 min/day + journaling)

· Romans 1–12 (1 chapter/day; journal Lie □ Truth □ Act).
· Matthew 5–7 (Sermon on the Mount; 1 section/day).
· John 1; 8; 14; Isaiah 53 (slow read; pray aloud).
· Hebrews 10–12 (copy two verses by hand).

90-Day Track (20–25 min/day + memory)
· Do the 60-Day plan plus:
· Memorize 6 anchors (see Memory Core).
· Weekly fast (one meal or one screen block).
· Family Mode once per week.

Memory Core—Twelve Verses that Rewire Reflexes

Identity & Renewal
· Romans 8:1—No condemnation in Christ.
· Romans 12:2—Renew your mind.
· Ephesians 2:10—His workmanship.
Truth & Freedom
· John 8:32—Truth sets free.
· John 14:6—Way, Truth, Life.
· Isaiah 53:5—By His wounds, healing.
Character & Speech
· Matthew 5:8—Pure in heart.
· Matthew 5:37—Yes be Yes.
Endurance & Discipline
· Hebrews 10:23—Hold fast hope.
· Hebrews 12:1–2—Run with endurance.
Self-control & Peace
· Galatians 5:16—Walk by the Spirit.
· Isaiah 26:3—Peace for the steadfast mind.

Countermeasures

When fear spikes:
· Psalm 27:1; Hebrews 13:5–6; Hebrews 12:1–2.
· Say the fear out loud; ask God for courage; take the smallest faithful step.

When lust knocks:
· Matthew 5:8; Galatians 5:16; Job 31:1.
· Change the room; change the device; pray out loud.
When anger surges:
· James 1:19–20; Matthew 5:22, 44–45.
· Pause two minutes; speak only what is true and necessary; bless once.
When despair whispers:
· Romans 8:31–39; Isaiah 40:28–31.
· Write one gratitude; serve once; text someone for prayer.
When pride swells:
· Philippians 2:3–8; Romans 12:3.
· Choose the lower seat; give unseen; confess one fault.
When confusion fogs:
· John 14:6; Romans 12:2; Proverbs 3:5–6.
· Stop scrolling; 10-minute Scripture walk; ask the next right obedience.

Guarding the Gate—Inputs Shape Instincts

· Add: 1 life-giving input (Psalm/Proverb; a sermon; wise long-form).
· Delete: 1 draining input (account, show, notification).
· Delay: 1 habit (phone stays out until Scripture + prayer).
· Defend: 1 window (tabletime no screens; last hour screen-free).

Family Mode—A Simple Home Rhythm

· Table (10 minutes): one verse, one question, one prayer.
· Bedtime (5 minutes): High / Low / Truth (one verse) + blessing.
· Weekly: serve once together; celebrate obedience; revisit boundaries.

Band of Two to Four

· Open: one verse aloud (Memory Core).
  · Report: Did / didn't; next act (one sentence each).
  · Repair: one pressure point; pray.
  · Resolve: one concrete obedience for the week.

Read When You Want to Quit

· Missed days? Start today. Formation beats perfection.
  · Feel nothing? Obey first; feelings follow faithfulness.
  · Home won't join? Lead quietly. Invite, don't nag.
  · Same stumble? Tighten gates; tell one trusted person; pair verse with a physical counteraction.

Quick Answers

· Can I swap passages? Yes—keep the four pillars (Foundation, Cross, Character, Perseverance).
  · How long daily? Start with 3–10 minutes. Grow if you want more.
  · New to faith? Great. Start with John 1 this week, Romans 8 next week.
  · Am I changing? Ask monthly: Are my reflexes truer? Are my inputs cleaner? Is my peace steadier?

Short Prayers

· Morning: Father, I belong to You. Renew my mind. Guard my gates. Lead me today. Amen.

· When Tempted: Jesus, You are truth. Set me free. I say no to this lesser thing and yes to You. Amen.

· When Angry: Lord, slow my mouth and steady my heart. Give me words that are true and necessary. Amen.

· Night: Thank You for today's mercies. Forgive my sins. Strengthen what is weak. Give me Your peace. Amen.

Closing Charge

You don't need permission—you've been commissioned. Open the Word. Expose the lie. Replace it with truth. Obey one thing today. Record it tonight. Repeat tomorrow. Homes don't drift toward order; they're steered there. Minds don't drift toward clarity; they're formed there. Legacies aren't accidents; they're forged by quiet, repeated choices.

"For we are His workmanship, created in Christ Jesus for good works ... that we should walk in them." (Ephesians 2:10)

After the Fire

My Journey to Faith

I: Growing Up in the Shadows

Introduction

W hen people ask me how I came to Christ, I always pause. Not because I don't know the answer, but because the journey isn't something you can sum up in a single sentence. It isn't just about the moment I prayed, or the day I first opened the Bible with seriousness. My journey has been one of shadows and light, of seeing darkness firsthand, of recognizing its counterfeit power, and of finally encountering the true King who rules over every spirit.

I grew up in a town where spiritual forces weren't abstract concepts to be debated in classrooms or whispered about in churches. They were everyday realities. Rituals, offerings, and strange ceremonies were woven into the culture like the air we breathed. People didn't question them; they accepted them as tradition, as part of who we were.

But even as a child, I could sense that something wasn't right.

The Atmosphere of My Town

The town I grew up in carried two very different faces. On one side, where most of the brujos lived, poverty clung like a shadow. Houses sagged in disrepair, the air felt heavy, and people walked with their heads down. Even though poverty existed across the whole country, there was something uniquely oppressive about that side of town. Outsiders avoided it unless they had business there, and even then they came and went quickly.

It wasn't just material poverty—it was spiritual. The streets were darker, the homes seemed colder, and joy was hard to find. There was a quiet fear that hung over that place, as though everyone knew they were walking under a weight they couldn't name.

But in the parts of town where churches gathered to worship Christ, everything felt different. I noticed it even before I knew Him. People still lived in small homes, they still worked hard and had little, but there was light in their eyes. They smiled more freely, and laughter seemed to spill into the streets. Even the air felt different—cleaner, fresher—as though it testified that something holy was present.

When I walked near a Christian church, I didn't have to guess which God was being worshiped—I could feel it. There was safety in those places, a peace that you couldn't find on the other side of town.

The Night I saw Possession

One night when I was still young, all the children in the neighborhood were invited to a gathering. To us, it was simple: there would be food, and that was enough reason to go. We weren't thinking about rituals, spirits, or power. We were thinking about plates of rice, meat, and sweet drinks we didn't always get at home.

I followed the others into the yard where the celebration was taking place. At first, it looked like a party—music, laughter, food. But then the drums started.

There was an old woman there, one I had seen many times before. She was frail, bent over, and could only move around with the help of her cane or walker. She was known in the neighborhood for her weakness, her fragile state. But as the drums pounded and the chanting grew louder, something changed.

She began to dance. At first, small steps. Then her movements became more wild, more powerful. Suddenly, she was leaping into the air—higher than athletes I'd later see on TV. Her eyes rolled back until only the whites showed. Her voice, normally weak, turned guttural and rough, a sound that didn't belong to her.

The crowd erupted in approval. To them, this was a sign of spiritual presence, a blessing. But to me, even as a child, it was frightening. It didn't feel holy; it felt heavy. The air itself seemed to shift, charged with something unnatural.

And then, as quickly as it began, it ended. The drums stopped, the chants faded, and the old woman returned to her chair. Her body was once again frail, her voice small, her steps halting and dependent on her walker.

It made no sense to me then. How could someone so weak leap like a young athlete? How could her voice transform into something inhuman? How could she have strength only while "possessed," and then collapse back into weakness the moment it was over?

I didn't know the answers, but I knew what I had seen was real. And I knew it wasn't good.

Scripture's Confirmation

Years later, when I finally gave my life to Christ and began reading the Bible with hungry eyes, that memory came rushing back to me. And suddenly, I understood.

The Bible had already described what I saw.

In Mark 5:2–4, a man possessed by many unclean spirits broke chains and could not be bound. His strength was unnatural, not his own. In Acts 16:16–18, a slave girl possessed by a spirit of divination followed Paul and Silas, shouting knowledge she shouldn't have had. Paul, in Jesus' name, commanded the spirit to leave, and it left instantly. And in Mark 9:17–27, a boy under the grip of a spirit convulsed, lost control of his body, and was tormented until Jesus commanded the spirit to depart.

What I had seen as a child wasn't culture, wasn't tradition, wasn't harmless. It was what Scripture warns about: unclean spirits using human bodies as vessels, showing counterfeit signs of power, and then leaving their victims weaker than before.

That old woman wasn't healed. She wasn't free. She was being used.

Food Offered to Idols

Another detail stands out when I look back. We, the children, were invited not just to watch but to eat from the offerings. At the time, it seemed like generosity. But when I later read 1 Corinthians 10:20–21, it shook me:

"The sacrifices of pagans are offered to demons, not to God, and I do not want you to be participants with demons. You cannot drink the cup of the Lord and the cup of demons too; you cannot have a part in both the Lord's table and the table of demons."

Paul's words described exactly what I had lived. The food was part of the ritual—by eating it, even unknowingly, children were being tied into something spiritual, something not of God. Yet even then, God was protecting me. I didn't know His name, but He already knew mine.

Looking back, I see two truths clearly: there is a kingdom of darkness active in this world, and Christ is greater. I didn't yet know Him personally that night, but years later the memory became more than confusion—it became confirmation. God had warned His people long ago about practices like these, and He was showing me that what I saw as a child wasn't imagination, but evidence of a larger spiritual battle.

And the most important truth of all? That battle has already been won.

II: The Encounter With a High Priest

A Season of Deep Devotion

By the time I crossed paths with him, my faith in Christ was burning strong. Prayer wasn't a duty—it was life. Scripture felt alive; worship spilled into mornings, work, and night. I wasn't looking for confrontation with darkness. I was providing for my family and walking closely with God. But walk nearer to the Light, and shadows reveal themselves clearly.

The Introduction

A client offered me a ride to pick up materials. When I stepped into his vehicle, something shifted. He looked at me with a kind of recognition—like he knew something about me before we spoke.

We talked about the project, then he glanced over. "You don't have to say it. I can see who you belong to."

I waited. Then said, "Yes. I belong to Christ."

He nodded, as if confirming a report. Then he said, almost casually, "Christ is God over all." Hearing truth from him didn't comfort me. It made me alert—like acknowledgment without surrender.

Who Spoke in the Car

His voice changed. He began speaking in tongues—words in an unknown language, rhythmic and charged. The air felt heavy, as if pressure filled the space. Yet fear never rose. Peace settled—the kind Jesus promised: "Peace I leave with you; my peace I give you... Do not let your hearts be troubled and do not be afraid" (John 14:27).

He finished with a long sigh and a smile, as if something had been accomplished. I knew better.

Secrets Spilled

He started talking about the rites he had endured to rise in his path—bones, tribal ceremonies, oaths that bound him to the powers he served. Then came the hook:

"If you ever need anything," he said, eyes on the road, "I'll be very happy to help you. Money. Protection. If enemies rise against you, I can make them disappear. Whatever you need."

It wasn't empty talk; there was weight behind it. But the offer was bait—an old lie in a new wrapper:

"Again, the devil took him to a very high mountain and showed him all the kingdoms... 'All this I will give you,' he said, 'if you will bow down and worship me.' Jesus said... 'Worship the Lord your God, and serve him only'" (Matthew 4:8–10).

Different seat, same temptation: promises of power in exchange for allegiance.

His Past

Without names, he sketched his history—advising powerful men, years in prison, then money, land, and a reputation that made some fear him and others revere him. But darkness is always recruiting; favors are just chains in disguise.

Covered by Christ

I didn't feel threatened because I wasn't alone. From the first moment he saw me, he knew whose I was. He said it himself: "I can see who you belong to."

"Submit yourselves, then, to God. Resist the devil, and he will flee from you" (James 4:7). I didn't argue or negotiate. My allegiance was already declared in heaven. Presence under Christ's authority speaks louder than counteroffers. And this remained true: "The one who is in you is greater than the one who is in the world" (1 John 4:4).

That car ride was a living parable. He offered what wasn't his to give. He revealed "mysteries" meant to impress, but they only exposed emptiness. Counterfeit power is noisy and transactional; Christ's power does not bargain. He speaks, and storms still.

I walked away grateful—covered by Christ, awake to the snare, and convinced again that every name bends beneath the name of Jesus.

III: Understanding the Counterfeit

Everyday Encounters With Darkness

Growing up, I saw things many would call superstition. To us, they were daily life.

I remember walking past certain houses and feeling heaviness before I reached the door. The air smelled of smoke and rum; outside the gates sat plates of food, half-burned cigars, or dead animals left as offerings. No one had to explain—we all knew.

A neighbor, desperate for healing, visited a practitioner who said she was cursed. She bathed in strange mixtures, left offerings at crossroads, and hid at home on nights "when spirits walked." For a moment she seemed lighter. Soon she was worse—anxious, fearful, convinced she was followed. She didn't find healing; she sank deeper into bondage.

Another man sought protection so enemies would fear him. For a time he carried himself like he had power. Then his marriage collapsed, his business fell, and his health crumbled. Whatever he thought he gained cost him far more.

These weren't rumors. They were my neighbors. The pattern was constant: a promise of freedom that ended in chains.

Why the Counterfeit Appeals

Poverty breeds desperation, and desperation makes almost anything look like hope: a promised cure when doctors can't name your illness; a charm for safety in a violent neighborhood; a ritual to rekindle a lost love; a rite to intimidate enemies. The pitch arrives as mercy—a shortcut to what your heart aches for. It can even bring a brief sense of relief. But it is credit, not gift, and the bill always comes due.

That's the bait. Darkness rarely begins with threats—it begins with promises, a shortcut to what the heart longs for. At first it can even seem to work. The bill comes later.

"There is a way that seems right to a man, but its end is the way to death." (Proverbs 14:12)

What seemed like healing brought deeper fear. What looked like power ended in ruin. What looked like freedom tightened into slavery.

The Mechanics of Rituals

The practices I saw depended on three pillars: possession, offerings, and oaths.

Possession ("mounting"): People believed spirits "rode" them, using their bodies. That's what I saw in the old woman—sudden strength, a strange voice, unnatural control. Not freedom—surrender of control.

Offerings and sacrifices: Food, drink, animals, and objects were left at crossroads, rivers, or altars. These were transactions meant to invite presence. Every offering was a contract—a debt.

Secrets and oaths: Initiates swore secrecy and performed rituals that bound them. The babalawo I met shared more than he should have; even his words carried the weight of oaths. These weren't harmless ceremonies—they were chains disguised as tradition.

For a little while, these pillars could produce effects—unnatural strength, temporary relief, false confidence. None of it lasted. The counterfeit cannot create; it only distorts.

The Bible's Warnings

Later, Scripture named exactly what I'd seen.

Leviticus 19:31—"Do not turn to mediums or seek out spiritists... you will be defiled by them."

Deuteronomy 18:10-12—forbids divination, sorcery, witchcraft, spells.

Isaiah 8:19-20—"Should not a people inquire of their God? Why consult the dead on behalf of the living?"

God isn't withholding power; He's protecting His people from slavery disguised as freedom.

And Jesus confronted the same spirits:

Mark 1:23-26—He drives out an impure spirit.

Luke 8:27-33—demons plead before Him, acknowledging His authority.

Every time—His word is enough. No chants, no bargaining—just authority.

False Healing vs. True Healing

The clearest difference is outcome.

The old woman seemed strong only while possessed; afterward she collapsed back into weakness. That wasn't healing—it was borrowed power at the cost of freedom.

Contrast Mark 5:25-34: a woman bleeding for twelve years touches Jesus' garment. She's healed instantly—physically, emotionally, spiritually. "Daughter, your faith has healed you... be freed from your suffering." Christ restores and gives peace; the counterfeit creates dependence on the next ritual.

Seeing these things made Scripture come alive. The warnings weren't distant—they explained what my eyes had already witnessed.

The counterfeit demands fear, secrecy, and sacrifice. Christ invites openly, frees without cost, and heals completely. The counterfeit enslaves by making you think you need it. Christ liberates by proving He is enough.

My encounters with Santería didn't just reveal its emptiness; they revealed Christ's fullness. Once you've seen the chains of the counterfeit, you understand how beautiful true freedom is.

IV: The Evidence of God in Creation

Before we dive in, hear my heart: this section isn't a crash course in astrophysics or biology. It's a glimpse into the trail of evidence that challenged me and ultimately convinced me that the signature of God is etched into the universe itself.

These aren't final answers. They're trail markers—the clues that pushed me to pray harder, study deeper, and wrestle longer.

If you're skeptical—good. You're exactly who I hope will read this. Consider Sir Lionel Luckhoo, a world-renowned trial attorney with a record-setting string of acquittals. He eventually applied the same courtroom logic to the historical claims of Jesus—and found them compelling. He didn't set aside reason to find faith. He followed the evidence to a verdict. That's the kind of thinking I respect.

So take this section as a compass, not a conclusion. Read widely. Verify claims. Ask hard questions. And then ask the hardest one: *What kind of world best explains the razor-sharp precision of the cosmos, the digital code in our DNA, the invisible laws that govern everything, and the stubborn facts of consciousness and morality?* If you let honest inquiry do its work, you may discover what I did: science doesn't shrink God—it sharpens the outline of His mind. It makes His voice in creation easier to hear.

Point 1: The Fine-Tuning of the Universe

Scientists have discovered something remarkable: the universe appears fine-tuned for life.

That means the fundamental constants and forces of nature are set at extremely precise values. Shift them ever so slightly—and you get a dead universe. No stars. No chemistry. No life. Not even atoms.

Let's look at a few examples:

Gravitational Constant ($G \approx 6.674 \times 10^{11}$): If gravity were slightly stronger, stars would burn out too quickly or collapse. If it were weaker, matter would never clump into galaxies or planets. The window for life is razor-thin—estimated around 1 in 10.

Cosmological Constant ($\approx 10^{122}$): This governs the expansion of the universe. Increase it just slightly—by about 1 part in 10^{12}—and galaxies never form. Decrease it—and the universe collapses in on itself.

Other ratios:

The ratio of the electromagnetic force to gravity (~10^{3})

The strength of the strong nuclear force ($\pm 2\%$ and atoms fall apart)

The mass ratio of electrons to protons (~$1/1836$)

Even tiny changes would destroy the building blocks of life.

Physicist Martin Rees identifies six key dimensionless numbers that must all fall within precise values to allow for a habitable universe. Roger Penrose calculated the odds of our universe's low-entropy beginning as 1 in $10^{\wedge}(10^{123})$—a number so large it defies imagination. Even Fred Hoyle, a once-skeptical astrophysicist, admitted the data *"suggests that a super-intellect has monkeyed with physics."*

Common Objections:

Multiverse?

No direct evidence exists. And even if it did, the "universe generator" would still need fine-tuned laws to produce life-permitting worlds.

Anthropic principle?
Saying "we observe this universe because we're here to observe it" may describe a selection effect, but it doesn't explain why the universe has the life-permitting conditions it does.

Necessity or chance?
Physics doesn't show these constants had to be this way. And pure "luck" at odds like 1 in $10^{(10^{123})}$ stretches the word beyond reason.

A Helpful Analogy:
Imagine picking one specific grain of sand—paint it red—have someone hide it somewhere in a Sahara-sized universe of sand. Then try to find it blindfolded.
The odds of that would be 1 in 10^{24}.

Now compare that to Λ's tuning, which is around 1 in 10^{120}. That's not just unlikely—it's incomprehensibly precise.

At some point, when the "impossible" keeps happening with precision, we stop calling it chance.
We call it design.

Why It Matters:
"The heavens declare the glory of God."
—Psalm 19:1
Fine-tuning isn't just about numbers.
It's about fingerprints.
Chance says "luck."
Faith says "love."

Point 2: The Mathematical Nature of Reality

Reality runs on a hidden grammar.

That grammar is mathematics—a language so precise, so predictive, and so elegant that it has become the foundation of every scientific advance since Newton. But here's the mystery: mathematics doesn't just describe what we observe. It *predicts* what we haven't yet seen.

A Tight Fit—Real Predictions
Throughout modern history, physicists have used pure math to predict phenomena long before they were observed:

James Clerk Maxwell's equations hinted at the existence of radio waves—years before they were detected.

Einstein's theory of general relativity predicted both gravitational lensing and gravitational waves—verified decades later with staggering accuracy.

Paul Dirac predicted the positron (antimatter) through a math equation, long before it was found in particle accelerators.

Erwin Schrödinger described quantum behavior not by accident, but by applying wave functions born from elegant equations.

The Higgs boson, neutrinos, and even Neptune were all first discovered *on paper*—not through a telescope, but through mathematical necessity.

This isn't coincidence. It's not retroactive. It's not projection.

It's discovery—fueled by logic, not luck.

Why Elegance Matters

In physics, beauty is often a clue. Equations that are simple, symmetrical, or elegant tend to be more predictive and powerful than those that are complex or clunky.

Physicists frequently say they "chase beauty" when searching for truth:

The geometry that describes gravity is Riemannian—curved and elegant. The Standard Model of particle physics relies on group theory—a stunningly symmetrical branch of mathematics. Quantum theory dances on the complex plane, using tools from complex analysis and linear algebra.

These aren't just tools for organizing data. They are *maps to reality*—and they consistently work.

This deep harmony led Nobel laureate Eugene Wigner to famously ask:

"Why is mathematics so unreasonably effective in the natural sciences?"

His question still haunts materialists.

But it makes perfect sense if reality was authored by a rational Mind—what Scripture calls the Logos:

"In the beginning was the Word [Logos]... and the Word was God... Through Him all things were made."
—John 1:1–3

Objection:

"Our brains evolved to spot patterns. That's why we see math everywhere."

This is a serious objection—and it deserves a fair response.

It's true that evolution favors pattern recognition. A brain that sees cause and effect has survival advantages: *This plant makes me sick. That shadow means danger. If I throw this spear like that, it hits the deer.*

But that level of pattern recognition doesn't require calculus. Or Lagrangian mechanics. Or tensor fields. Or imaginary numbers. Or Hilbert spaces. Or string theory.

Spear-throwing doesn't explain the human mind's ability to describe quantum entanglement using matrix algebra.
Or to simulate black hole collisions using differential geometry.

Put plainly: our minds are wildly over-equipped for mere survival.

Evolution explains why we might find patterns. It doesn't explain why the patterns themselves are real, stable, and deeply mathematical.

Nor does it explain why abstract math created in the human mind somehow matches the deep structures of the cosmos.
We invented imaginary numbers in the 1500s—and centuries later, they turned out to be central to quantum physics.

At some point, it's more reasonable to conclude that the universe runs on logic because it was designed by Logic.

I don't worship math.
But sometimes, when I stare at a whiteboard full of equations—or run my hand over the edge of a diagram—I feel something deeper than pattern.

I sense mind. Order. Intent.
Not random syntax, but *sentence.* Not chaos, but code.
Not just math that works, but math that sings.

"God is not a God of confusion, but of order."
—1 Corinthians 14:33

The deeper I study the grammar of the universe, the clearer the voice becomes.

I don't worship equations. I worship the Mind behind them.

Point 3: The Origin of the Universe

The universe hasn't always existed.

That's not speculation. It's the best-supported conclusion of modern cosmology.

If you follow the expansion of the universe backward, you don't get a gentle fade into eternity—you hit a beginning. A moment when time, space, matter, and energy all came into being.

And whatever begins... has a cause.

Lines of Evidence

Multiple scientific discoveries converge on the same point: the universe is not eternal.

Hubble's redshift measurements (1920s) revealed that galaxies are moving away from us—meaning the universe is expanding.

In 1965, the discovery of the Cosmic Microwave Background (CMB) provided powerful confirmation of a hot, dense early state.

The precise abundances of light elements—hydrogen, helium, and lithium—match the predictions of a universe that expanded and cooled after a sudden origin.

Modern satellites like WMAP and Planck have mapped the CMB with incredible precision, pointing to a universe that began around 13.8 billion years ago.

Then there's the Borde-Guth-Vilenkin (BGV) theorem, a critical result in cosmology. It shows that any universe which is, on average, expanding—like ours—cannot be past-infinite. There must be a beginning.

As physicist Alexander Vilenkin himself said:

"*All the evidence we have says that the universe had a beginning.*"

JWST's Early-Universe Surprise

When the James Webb Space Telescope (JWST) launched, scientists expected to find young, chaotic galaxies in the early universe. Instead, it found mature, structured galaxies far earlier than expected—some less than 300 million years after the Big Bang.

It's like expecting to find scaffolding and construction dust... and instead seeing finished skyscrapers.

This compression of cosmic timelines hints at something deeper—front-loaded order, not random chaos. The fingerprints of intention, not just inertia.

Kalam in Plain Terms

One of the simplest—and most compelling—philosophical arguments for a Creator is the Kalam Cosmological Argument:

Whatever begins to exist has a cause. The universe began to exist. Therefore, the universe has a cause. But this isn't just cold logic. The nature of that cause must match what came into being:

Timeless—because time itself began at the Big Bang.

Spaceless—because space was created too.

Immaterial—not made of matter or energy.

Immensely powerful—to bring the entire cosmos into existence.

And **personal**—because impersonal forces don't make choices; a will is needed to decide *when* creation begins.

The first sentence of Scripture now rhymes with modern cosmology:

"*In the beginning, God created the heavens and the earth.*"—Genesis 1:1

"*By faith we understand that the universe was created by the word of God...*"—Hebrews 11:3

Objection:

"Quantum physics shows something can come from nothing. So we don't need God to explain the beginning."

This idea became popular after physicist Lawrence Krauss wrote A *Universe from Nothing*. But there's a problem: his "nothing" isn't really nothing. When scientists speak of quantum "nothing," they often mean a vacuum state—a low-energy field governed by physical laws. This "nothing" still contains:

Quantum fields

The laws of physics

Spacetime itself

In other words, it's not nothing in the philosophical sense—it's a something with structure and rules. Imagine you walk into a dark room and hear music playing. If someone told you, "Oh, that's just coming from nothing," you'd rightly ask: *Nothing? Or hidden speakers and a power source?* Other proposed models—like cyclic universes or quantum bounce scenarios—run into similar walls. Cyclic models face increasing entropy (disorder) with each cycle, which eventually makes the process unsustainable. And chance from nothing ends up redefining "nothing" into "something random," which dodges the real issue.

Even atheists like Sean Carroll admit: we have no working model that explains the origin of the universe without assumptions—assumptions that themselves beg for explanation.

At some point, the honest thinker has to ask: *Why is there something rather than nothing?*

The fact that anything exists at all is not trivial. It's not just a scientific question. It's a personal one.

Where did all of this come from? Why is there something rather than nothing? And why does that "something" make sense, hold together, and support life? The Big Bang isn't the enemy of faith. It's one of its strongest witnesses. "In the beginning..." isn't a metaphor.

It's a fingerprint.

Existence itself points beyond itself.

Point 4: DNA Complexity and Information

Inside every cell is more than chemistry—there's code.

DNA is digital: it stores, copies, edits, and translates information using a four-letter alphabet. Molecular machines called polymerases proofread with remarkable accuracy—just one error in every billion bases. Ribosomes read the code and build proteins with help from tRNA "delivery trucks" and synthetases that double-check for accuracy.

Cells don't just carry instructions—they execute them with precision, coordination, and error correction.

The density is staggering: DNA can store about 1 million gigabytes per gram, with overlapping instructions and near-optimal design to reduce mutation risk. And inside are nanoscale engines like ATP synthase turbines and bacterial flagellar motors—systems that must be built and aligned *together* to function at all.

The Real Problem

Evolution can tweak existing code. But it doesn't explain how the first coded system came to be.

Even RNA-world theories still require a working sequence, a stable environment, and a decoding system—all showing up at once.

Why Chance Falls Short

A typical protein has 150 amino acids. That's $10^{1\square\square}$ possible combinations—but functional sequences are incredibly rare (around 1 in $10\square\square$). That's like finding one coherent sentence in a library of gibberish, and then needing *multiple* such sentences to work *together*.

Chance isn't a creator. It's just a placeholder.

Objection:

"You're just filling a gap in knowledge. We don't know everything about abiogenesis."

True—we don't. And science should keep searching.

But this isn't about missing data. It's about information—which is not produced by chemistry alone. Just like ink doesn't create the message, molecules don't create meaning. At some point, you need a mind to assign rules, build systems, and carry out instructions.

"I praise You, for I am fearfully and wonderfully made."—Ps alm 139:14

DNA isn't noise. It's language.

You are not random. You are written.

Point 5: Abstract Laws (Logic, Morality, Math)

Some truths are invisible—but undeniable.

Logic, morality, and mathematics are not material things. You can't weigh them or bottle them. Yet they govern everything from equations to ethics, from courtrooms to calculus.

They are immaterial, universal, and binding.

Materialism's Tension

If reality is just atoms and energy, where do abstract laws come from?

No arrangement of molecules explains why "A cannot equal not-A."

No chemical reaction produces the concept of prime numbers.

And no evolutionary urge explains why we say "torturing children is wrong," even when it offers no survival advantage.

If math is just a human invention, why does it work on galaxies we've never touched? If morality is just survival instinct, why do we admire those who die protecting strangers? We live as though truth, order, and goodness are real—and not just personal preferences.

The Moral Argument

If God does not exist, objective moral duties do not exist. But objective moral duties do exist. Therefore, God exists. We might disagree on moral details, but across time and culture, some things are recognized as *truly* wrong—rape, murder, cruelty for pleasure. Not just inconvenient. Wrong.

That points beyond us.

Biblical Resonance

The law is written on the human heart (Romans 2:14–15). God is a God of order, not chaos (1 Corinthians 14:33). Christ is the **Logos**—the rational foundation of all things (John 1:1).

A Helpful Analogy

Chess pieces are physical. But the rules of chess are not. They're abstract, yet they govern every move. The universe plays by rules, too—logical, moral, and mathematical. And rules imply a Rule-giver.

We use reason, live by moral instinct, and trust math daily. But if there's no Mind behind the universe, we're borrowing tools from a worldview we claim to reject. We reason with the mind of God—even when we deny Him.

Point 6: Human Consciousness and Moral Awareness

Your brain may fire neurons, but *you* feel grief. You love. You contemplate meaning. These are not illusions—they are first-person experiences, what philosophers call *qualia*. They don't reduce to molecules, and no lab instrument has ever measured the ache of loss or the thrill of music. Materialism explains behavior; it doesn't explain experience.

Philosopher David Chalmers famously pointed out that even if we mapped every brain process, we'd still be missing the central mystery: why it feels like something to be you. Color, pain, longing, conviction—none of these are visible under a microscope, yet they define our inner life. If thoughts are merely neural noise, why should we trust them as true? As C.S. Lewis warned, if our reasoning is a cosmic accident, then the conclusions we reach—including that very idea—are suspect. Wind in the trees can make noise, but it doesn't *think*.

This brings us to morality: we don't only *feel*—we *evaluate*. We call certain things truly wrong. We recoil at abuse, no matter where it happens, and we admire sacrifice, no matter the cost. Evolutionary theory can account for cooperation that helps a group survive, but it struggles to explain why someone would throw themselves on a grenade for strangers. It also can't fully account for guilt when no one is watching, or why we recognize some acts as evil—not merely inconvenient.

The Bible speaks directly to this inner life. Genesis says we were made in the image of God—not just biological beings, but moral agents. Ecclesiastes says eternity is set in the human heart. Romans says our conscience bears witness. Christianity doesn't just match biology—it *explains the human experience*, including the tension we feel between what we are and what we sense we were meant to be.

Some skeptics argue that consciousness will eventually be explained through neuroscience. And science has certainly found correlations between brain activity and mental states. But correlation isn't identity. A guitar string may vibrate, but the music comes from the player. Likewise, brain activity may support thought, but it doesn't explain the "I" that thinks. Even atheists like Thomas Nagel admit this remains a gaping hole in materialist explanations.

You are not a machine. You are not an illusion. You are a soul—with reason, memory, desire, and moral weight. And when you say "I," you are naming something that atoms cannot account for. The inner world of the human person is one of the most powerful clues that something more is going on. As Scripture says, "For what can be known about God is plain... His invisible attributes... have been clearly perceived" (Romans 1:19–20).

One Harmony: The Voice in Stereo

Taken alone, each point may seem interesting or even abstract. But taken together—fine-tuning, mathematical structure, a cosmic beginning, digital information in DNA, immaterial moral law, and conscious self-awareness—they form a cumulative case: a world that bears the fingerprints of a personal Mind.

These arguments didn't create my faith. Christ did. But they anchored it. They reminded me that truth isn't afraid of scrutiny. That the same God who spoke through Scripture also spoke through the structure of creation. That the Author of nature and the Author of salvation are one and the same.

Study the universe. Study the Word. Study your own heart. You'll find the same voice whispering through all three.

The Author of Scripture is the Author of nature.

Learn to listen—and you'll hear Him in stereo.

V: Christ's Authority Over Every Spirit

Introduction: Why Authority Matters
In earlier chapters, I unpacked the counterfeit systems I grew up around—Santería, brujería, and the empty promises they made. I also walked through the rational evidence for God in creation: fine-tuning, mathematics, the origin of the universe, DNA, abstract laws, and human consciousness. These ideas matter—especially for skeptics and seekers. But faith can't live on arguments alone. Life isn't just about what we think—it's about what we live.

This is where authority enters. The world is full of spirits and systems that offer power, shortcuts, protection, and healing. But most are deceptive, and all are temporary. The real question isn't just whether God exists, but who has true authority over life, death, and the unseen. Scripture answers clearly: Christ reigns supreme.

The Biblical Witness of Authority
When Jesus entered the synagogue in Capernaum, people were stunned—not just by His teaching, but by the weight of His words. A man with an impure spirit cried out, "What do you want with us, Jesus of Nazareth?... I know who you are—the Holy One of God!" Jesus commanded, "Be quiet! Come out of him!" and the spirit obeyed. The crowd asked, "What is this? A new teaching—and with authority! Even the impure spirits obey him" (Mark 1:24–27).

Throughout the Gospels, demons recognized Jesus before most people did. In Luke 8, the legion of spirits inside the Gerasene man begged Him not to send them into the abyss. Even evil knows where its limits lie. And that same authority wasn't hoarded—it was shared. Jesus told His followers, "I have given you authority... to overcome all the power of the enemy" (Luke 10:19). The apostles lived it. Paul cast out spirits in Acts 16. In Acts 19, demons acknowledged Jesus' authority even when false exorcists tried to invoke His name.

Scripture speaks with one voice: Christ holds all authority—above every spirit, every ruler, every realm.

False Power vs. True Power

Counterfeit power can impress. But it cannot save. It enslaves more than it frees, and always takes more than it gives. Only Christ brings life, truth, and freedom. When I encountered that babalawo years later, his expression changed the moment he saw me. He knew I belonged to Christ before I said a word. That moment wasn't about me. It was about the seal of Christ that speaks louder than fear.

The Christian's Position in Christ

There's deep comfort in knowing the authority Jesus carried has been extended to His people. First John says, "Greater is He who is in you than he who is in the world." Ephesians tells us to "be strong in the Lord and in His mighty power." And Luke 10:19 reminds us that our position in Christ gives authority over the forces that once intimidated us.

This doesn't mean we won't face struggle. Paul said we wrestle against spiritual forces. But we fight from a position of victory, not fear. Christ's resurrection disarmed every principality (Colossians 2:15). Christians have no need to fear brujería, curses, or rituals. They might terrify those outside of Christ—but for those in Him, they're empty threats. No curse can override a life covered by the blood of the Lamb.

Testimony: Living Under Christ's Authority

I've walked through neighborhoods where brujería was practiced openly. You can feel the heaviness, the fear. But I've also walked through places where Christ is worshiped, and the difference is tangible—light in the air, peace in the people, joy that lingers. It reminds me of Acts 8, where Philip preached in a city once held captive by a sorcerer named Simon. When the true power of Christ arrived, the counterfeit collapsed.

In my own life, people have tried to intimidate me spiritually. But I've never felt shaken—not because I'm strong, but because I know who I belong to. Authority doesn't come from shouting or performing rituals. It comes from being united with the One who reigns over all.

Christ Reigns Supreme

In the end, every spirit bows to Christ. Philippians says that at the name of Jesus, every knee will bow—in heaven, on earth, and under the earth—and every tongue will confess that Jesus Christ is Lord. That includes demons, rulers, skeptics, and occultists. No power outranks His name.

So here's the call: don't settle for counterfeits. Don't bow to fear. Don't trade your future for a shortcut. Follow the One whose authority is absolute, whose love is perfect, and whose victory is eternal.

For me, this has been the heart of my journey. I grew up surrounded by spiritual confusion. I was offered power by spirits that do not love us. But I came to know the One who does. From brujería to belief, from false promises to the Word made flesh—this much I know:

Christ reigns.

And when you belong to Him, you walk in the shadow of the only true authority.

VI: Conclusion—From Darkness to Light

Recap of the Journey

As I look back on everything I've shared in these pages, I see a clear thread running through it all. I began in a world shaped by superstition—Santería, brujería, and the counterfeit power they promised. I witnessed possession with my own eyes: an old woman leaping with unnatural strength, her voice changed, her gaze hollow. I sat across from a babalawo who whispered secrets and offered favors in exchange for allegiance.

But through it all, Christ was calling me. Even before I could name His voice, He was guarding my steps. When counterfeit spirits tried to impress me, Christ reminded me who He was. When shortcuts appeared, He pointed me to the narrow road that leads to life.

Later, I discovered that the God who rescued me spiritually also revealed Himself in creation. I studied the fine-tuning of the universe, the elegance of math, the beginning of time, the complexity of DNA, the reality of abstract laws, and the mystery of consciousness. And in all of it, I found not randomness—but reason. Not silence—but design. Not confusion—but a Creator.

And I came to see that the same Christ who holds galaxies in place holds authority over every spirit. Every demon, every lie, every counterfeit power must bow. He alone is Lord.

What It Means for You, the Reader

This book isn't just about my story. It's an invitation to consider your own.

– **Discern the counterfeit.** The world is full of promises—some spiritual, some material. They may glitter, but they enslave. Don't fall for shadows when truth is within reach.

– **Embrace the evidence.** You don't have to choose between faith and reason. The book of nature and the Word of God speak with one voice. Don't let anyone convince you belief is blind—it's the clearest vision there is.

– **Trust the authority.** In Christ, you have nothing to fear—not curses, not rituals, not darkness. His authority is final. And when you belong to Him, you walk in freedom.

A Call to Decision

Faith is more than information—it is transformation, and transformation begins with a choice.

Joshua stood before Israel and said, "Choose this day whom you will serve... but as for me and my household, we will serve the Lord" (Joshua 24:15). That choice still stands.

Jesus said, "I am the way and the truth and the life. No one comes to the Father except through Me" (John 14:6). Paul put it simply: "If you declare with your mouth, 'Jesus is Lord,' and believe in your heart that God raised Him from the dead, you will be saved" (Romans 10:9).

No ritual, no charm, no possession can save you. Only Christ can. The question is—will you choose Him?

Encouragement for Believers

If you already belong to Christ, let this chapter remind you of what's true. You do not walk in fear. The darkness may roar, but it cannot overcome the light.

– *You are sealed.* "When you believed, you were marked in Him with a seal, the promised Holy Spirit" (Ephesians 1:13).
– *You are protected.* "Greater is He who is in you than he who is in the world" (1 John 4:4).
– *You are equipped.* "Put on the full armor of God..." (Ephesians 6:11).

So live with confidence. Walk in freedom. Speak truth boldly. Let your life shine light in every place where shadows remain.

Final Reflection: Gratitude

I close this book with deep gratitude: to God, who pulled me out of counterfeit darkness and set my feet on solid ground; to His Word, which proves itself true through both Scripture and science; to my family, who walk this path with me; and most of all, to my son—for whom much of this was written. May you not only read about faith, but live it.

My prayer is that you, too, will hear the voice of Christ, recognize the evidence of His fingerprints, and trust His authority over every power—that you will step out of the shadows and into His marvelous light.

Because in the end, this story isn't just about leaving Santería. It's not just about answering skeptics. It's about this:

Christ is King. He reigns.

And when you belong to Him, you have nothing to fear.

Author Note

A Witness to the Forge

E very book is born out of a journey, and this one is no different. But if you've made it to these final pages, you deserve the honest version: Forge the Mind is not simply the product of willpower, study, or a steady pen. Those are tools in my hands, but the spark inside the furnace is Christ—the One who found me long before I ever reached for Him. This isn't a book about me, yet it would be dishonest to hide the testimony behind the pages. A witness is only useful if he speaks.

I wasn't raised expecting ease, and life never offered illusions of comfort. My story is a patchwork of countries and trades, late nights and early mornings. I've worn work gloves as an electrician, boots as a renovator, the weight of a father, and the mantle of a head of household. I've trained my body with sweat and lifted more than steel: the burden of provision, the discipline of study, and the demand to stand upright in a world that prefers you soft. None of these are complaints. They are gifts—because they taught me that the end of my strength is the beginning of Christ's.

For years I hunted truth like a man crossing desert ground for water. I studied science and technology—not as escapes, but as windows into the order God wrote into creation. I wrestled with philosophy to test the ideas that parade as wisdom in our age. I trained in fitness to tell my body it wasn't in charge. I walked the road of stoicism and respected its call to composure under fire, but I found its border: it can steady the will; it cannot save the soul. The forge can temper a blade; only the Maker gives it purpose.

Scripture stopped being a scattered set of verses and became a kit I could fight with. What emerged wasn't a coffee-mug list; it was a battle-ready canon. Romans for the foundation of salvation and truth, John and Isaiah for the identity and sacrifice of Christ, Matthew 5 for the culture of the Kingdom, and Hebrews for grit and perseverance. That list isn't random; it's a soldier's list. It gives the spine to this book: doctrine over comfort, confrontation with sin, the cross at the center, transformation that lasts, and endurance when the weather turns. If you trace those anchors, you can see the shape of my theology—and the training program this book has been inviting you into.

It was the words of Jesus that cut through the noise and the fortresses I'd built. He didn't offer moral tips; He spoke reality. "You will know the truth, and the truth will set you free." That verse never left me because it revealed the difference between behavior management and transformation. I could change habits; only Christ could change a heart. Forge the Mind is about that difference—training a mind to stand because a soul has bowed to the right King.

I don't write as a scholar living above real life. I write as a man who has met deadlines with ache in his back and prayer on his lips. I write as a husband learning that love is covenant, not sentiment. I write as a father who knows children imitate more than they obey. I write as a believer convinced grace is not light—it's blood-bought. If my words are sharp, it's because flattery makes dull tools. If they are tender, it's because I've needed mercy more than once.

So let me be clear about who's behind these pages and who isn't. Why a testimony instead of a résumé? Because careers and achievements vanish at the grave. The question that matters isn't what I can build with my hands, but what I'm letting Christ build in my inner life. If you finish this book and remember nothing about me except that I tried to point you to Jesus and to a life aligned with truth, that will be success enough.

Still, clarity matters. My calling is twofold: I build homes and I build words. One labor repairs what people can see; the other aims at what only God sees. Both require integrity. When I drive a nail, I refuse shortcuts because a family will live with my choices. When I write, I refuse to sand down truth because a reader's soul might lean on these beams. Both crafts share one law: alignment.

I have been shaped by contrasts. I appreciate scientific rigor yet refuse to trade Scripture's wisdom for cultural applause. I respect philosophy's questions yet kneel before revelation's answers. I've admired strong men yet learned to boast only in weakness so Christ gets the glory. These tensions don't dilute faith—they purify it. Christianity isn't a crutch for the naïve; it's the cross the proud must carry if they would truly live. And this book is a field manual for carrying it with a clear mind in a loud age.

Why write Forge the Mind when the shelves already sag with Self-Help and Spirituality? Because our generation is drowning in information and starving for formation. Stoicism can steady your breath in the storm; it cannot tell the sea to be still. Therapy can name the wound; only Christ heals to the bone. We need something older and stronger than trend, and someone more faithful than our feelings. We need Christ—and the disciplined, clear, obedient mind that follows Him into the noise and refuses to bow.

This is not a book about perfection. It's a book about preparation. A steady mind isn't born by accident; it's forged by truth. That means practices, not platitudes. It means boundaries around your inputs, training for your will, repentance when you drift, and courage when you must stand alone. It means learning to take thoughts captive, to mute clamor that weakens you, to prefer clarity over comfort, to pick conviction over performance. It means building inner order because God is a God of order, and planting your feet on the Rock so the storm can teach you but never own you.

Some will read this as a challenge to men. It is. But it is also an invitation for every soul—son or daughter, single or married, believer or skeptic—who is tired of drifting and ready to build. If you're skeptical, you're not my enemy; you're my reader. I'm not here by pedigree or platform. I'm here because Jesus interrupted my life, re-ordered my loves, and handed me words I couldn't keep to myself. If they help you see Him more clearly and live more firmly, then the forge did its work.

I won't pretend to know every turn ahead. The future is a road with fog and light in shifting measure. But I know this: every page you just read, every verse I've clung to, every habit I've rebuilt, every nail I've set straight, every apology I've owed and paid—each belongs to the same end: that Christ would be formed in me, and, by God's mercy, in you. That your mind would become a gate guarded by truth. That your will would learn obedience under pressure. That your peace would be something the world can neither give nor steal.

If you want to know the author, know the Savior he serves. Apart from Him, I am nothing more than a man with tools and intentions. With Him, I am a witness to grace, to truth, and to the kind of inner strength this world cannot counterfeit.

Now close the book the right way: not with admiration, but with obedience. Take one practice from these pages and make it a rule of life. Tell one trusted person what you're building. Set a date to review your discipline. And when you fail—because every man does—return quickly to repentance, recalibrate, and keep walking.

The fire will still be hot out there. The anvil will still be sure. And the Smith will still be kind.

Acknowledgements

No mind is forged in isolation. Every truth here was tested in the fire of others' wisdom and doubt. To those who questioned my drafts and challenged my arguments—your resistance shaped the steel.

To my family, who gave me time when time was costly, and grace when the process ran long.

To my son—you are the reason I chose discipline over ease, and clarity over applause. This book carries your name between its lines.

To the craftsmen, teachers, and thinkers who taught me that strength and wisdom are not opposites but allies—your example gave these pages their backbone.

And to God, the Architect of reason and redemption—every good line returns to You.

Books That Shaped The Forge

Wisdom is not inherited; it's discovered in the words of those who walked before us. These are the books that strengthened my foundations and may strengthen yours.

Scripture
- *The Holy Bible*—Foundation and compass

Faith & Moral Reason
- *Mere Christianity* (C.S. Lewis)
- *The Abolition of Man* (C.S. Lewis)
- *The Case for Christ* (Lee Strobel)
- *More Than a Carpenter* (Josh McDowell)
- *The Prince of Peace* (Coming Soon)

Philosophy & Virtue
- *Meditations* (Marcus Aurelius)
- *The Discourses & Enchiridion* (Epictetus)
- *Letters from a Stoic* (Seneca)
- *Man's Search for Meaning* (Viktor E. Frankl)

Discipline & Endurance
- *Can't Hurt Me* (David Goggins)
- *The War of Art* (Steven Pressfield)
- *12 Rules for Life* (Jordan B. Peterson)

www.ingramcontent.com/pod-product-compliance
Lightning Source LLC
Chambersburg PA
CBHW022052020426
42335CB00012B/658